Forbes Macgregor was born ·-
educated in the city and in :
London University by private
a scoutmaster in the Canonga
and camping all over Scotlanc

In 1924 he started a teachii
one years and ended in 1965 ᵥ
of South Morningside Primary

He was the author of num.   Grey-
friars Bobby: The Real Story at La   20   12682831   6318   *ymes*,
Famous Scots, *Macgregor's Mixture* and *More Macgregor's Mixture*.

Forbes Macgregor died in 1991.

BY THE SAME AUTHOR

Forbes Macgregor

Clan Gregor

Steve Savage
LONDON AND EDINBURGH

Steve Savage Publishers Ltd
The Old Truman Brewery
91 Brick Lane
LONDON
E1 6QL

www.savagepublishers.com

Published in paperback by Steve Savage Publishers Ltd 2012
First published in Great Britain by The Clan Gregor Society 1977
Copyright © Forbes Macgregor 1977

ISBN: 978-1-904246-37-4

Typeset by Steve Savage Publishers
Printed and bound by SRP Ltd, Exeter

Contents

Introduction

American MacGregors celebrate bi-centenary – Clan Gregor Society – Old tradition endures – Difficulty of realising the past.

Much Scottish history fabulous – A true history of Clan Gregor never written – Our Celtic forebears – Three atrocities in the North – Unchanging character of Caledonians.

MacGregors regarded as naturally wicked – The Highlands' opposite view – Dr. Johnson's prejudice caused by the behaviour of David Mallet (a MacGregor in London).

Sir Walter Scott knew the truth – Published *Rob Roy* – Other vindications of Rob Roy – Scott's sympathies with MacGregors – A suggestion about a 'Scott Supper' annually.

Part 1. Origins.

Hallowed tradition – Inflated kinglets – Several Alpins, kings of Picts – Treachery of Alpin, son of Hugh the Poisonous.

The Scottish records vandalised – Celtic snake-pit – Kenneth MacAlpin's shotgun wedding.

Preface to the 1997 Edition

For many years Forbes Macgregor was regarded as a father figure of the clan in Scotland and also of the Clan Gregor Society worldwide. He and his wife Jean took an active part in Society affairs and were ever present at functions including annual gatherings and the Lochearnhead Balquhidder and Strathyre Highland Games, which for many years Society members have traditionally attended.

Down through the centuries much has appeared in print about Clan Gregor. Material ranges from *The Book of the Dean of Lismore*, our earliest extant Collection of Gaelic Poetry, through the miscellaneous records to be had in archives in Edinburgh, Stirling and elsewhere, the documentary of the Clan Gregor, 2 volumes, published nearly a century ago, to studies of the lives of individual MacGregors, most notably Rob Roy.

As a writer Forbes MacGregor had long felt a desire to write about his Clan in a work which would bring together many facets of its long and distinguished history, and in a way which would appeal to the average reader. His book was completed in the mid-seventies and was duly published by the Clan Gregor Society in 1977. Since then copies have sold steadily and, as the Society continued to grow in the 1980s and 1990s the number of copies in stock dwindled. In 1996 since there were few copies remaining, the Society, with the permission of Forbes's widow Jean, decided to reprint his book and has been proud to do so.

As ever the book is thoroughly recommended. It is easily read, full of anecdotes and is never dull.

The Society is aware that on-going research by members of the Clan has extended our knowledge of the history of Clan

Gregor since Forbes wrote, but prefers to offer the book in its original form as a memento to Forbes.

Sadly, Forbes died in 1991, but may this history of Clan Gregor ever serve as a memorial to a very fine and worthy gentleman.

Forbes Macgregor.

The Council and Members of the Clan Gregor Society.
11 December 1996.

A book written with regard for truth
and in no awe of Caesar.

Of Old Things we write something new,
if Truth may receive addition.

Sir Thomas Browne

Author's Apology

I have been encouraged in several ways to write the history of my clan, not the least influential of which was the impression made on me, by a lifetime of reading Scottish history, that, in the phrase of Joseph Anderson, Curator of the Scottish National Museum of Antiquities, written in 1890, 'the true story of the doings and sufferings of this devoted clan has yet to be dug from the dry-as-dust sources of historical contemporary records'. Several assemblages of stories and records of the clan have been published before and after 1890, more or less reliable and readable; but a true story covering several centuries and involving innumerable families and individuals is more than the sum of its parts, and I do not think such a work is within the power of a single pen. I must compromise to the extent of making a shorter version which is not so condensed as to be a mere catalogue, but which is enlivened by incidents from picturesque MacGregor history, or tradition, and by my own comments, guided by a respect for Truth and an irreverence for Caesar, all set in the long historical framework of the Christian era.

It could be objected that a MacGregor is not the proper person to write a history of his own people as he is almost certainly obliged to bring innate prejudice to the task. I admit, in the light of some MacGregor histories I have read, that there are grounds for this objection and that, in the history of some Highland Clans now on sale, only a fraction have been written by actual clan members. Although I think Oscar Wilde hit the mark when he said that unbiased evidence was worthless, yet I have been on my guard against writing a prejudiced story, and I put my reader on the alert now, to look out for any propaganda in this book. On the other hand, who is better placed to tell the true human story of his people than one of their blood and inheritance? Can anyone reasonably object to the character of the Bible because, with the possible exception of the book of Job, it was written by Jewish authors? Or, to come nearer to this day and age, who can deny the testimony of the American Indians and communities of Pacific islanders, as to the cynically harsh treatment they continue to endure from white administrators?

This is an increasingly critical age of revolt by human groups who have been long passive and dumb, and there are too many wrongs to be righted for anyone to be roused to any real extent by the injustices suffered by a small clan of Scottish people during the late mediaeval and early modern times, and which were legally put right exactly two centuries ago.

One of the most comprehensible sayings of Hegel the philosopher is, 'what experience and history teach is this – that people and governments have never learned anything from history, or acted on principles deduced from it.' If this is true, then the story of Clan Gregor will not be a guidance or a warning for the present, or any other day; but it should be of interest to all members, and to Highland clansmen and clanswomen over the wide world, for it is to a large extent the story of all the Celtic people in their clash with an antagonistic political system.

It is normal practice for MacGregors to provide some data on their own family ancestry. I cannot go back with certainty before the middle of the eighteenth century, but I have checked the records of Aberlour and of Knockando parishes in Strathspey and noted that my great-great-grandfather died, an aged man, in Bruntlands Farm, Knockando, in 1833, and that his son James was born in Upper Ringorum Farm on 28th December 1789: and, from family records, that son, James, my great-grandfather, died at 46 Eglinton Street, Gorbals parish, Glasgow in 1852; his son David, my paternal grandfather, was born at the above address in 1831 and died in Doncaster, Yorks, in 1924; my father David was born in Dumfries in the house now known as Burns' House, in 1863, and died at Clynder, Gareloch on April 18th, 1910. I was born in Edinburgh on July 13th, 1904.

There are now no descendants of my MacGregor forebears in Aberlour or Knockando. There is a tradition, which may be verified from various sources, that Rob Roy, when a young man of about twenty, came to the aid of Patrick Grant, a flamboyant local chieftain, about 1690, and left two strong runners in Speyside to bear word to Rob should the MacIntoshes annoy Grant. In the parish records I found that the name MacGregor occurred first in 1741, when a child John was born in Carron to Alexander McGrigor, after which there were occasional entries in and around Carron and Archiestown until about 1890. All these appear to have been descendants of the 'planted' runners. Most of my ancestors belonged to the 'New Lichts' or Associate Synod and were not due to be recorded by the Established Church. Nevertheless their gravestones are in Aberlour.

Introduction

1. *Two Centuries since the Name was Restored.*

In 1975, the bi-centenary of the Repeal of the Acts of Proscription against Clan Gregor, a large party of American MacGregors, which also included citizens of Mexico, spent a fortnight in Scotland revisiting the localities famous in Highland and particularly in MacGregor history. In those two centuries since the return of the clan to legal existence its members have been conspicuous in all fields of human endeavour, either in the arts of peace or war. But the clan, as a Celtic entity, ceased to exist after 1747, when legislation destroyed the basis of the system, and the MacGregors, like all other Highland clans, had to continue their distinctive existence as a social body, or society. The Clan Gregor Society has been in more or less active existence since it was brought into being shortly after the rather hectic summer of 1822 when, chiefly at the instigation of Sir Walter Scott, King George IV visited Scotland, and the whole nation, with the exception of Thomas Carlyle and kindred cynics, sported the tartan, whether or not they had a drop of Highland blood. Ever since that saturnalia in Edinburgh, Highland Clan Societies have flourished, Highland Games have been revived, and piping contests arranged, though it may be noted that the latter had been held in many parts of Britain, including London, for some years before. A general proscription on all things Highland was enforced after the Forty-five rising, and it was not lifted until 1782: nevertheless at the Falkirk Tryst, the greatest market of sheep and cattle in Britain and, of course, a huge gathering of clansmen, the piping contest was won by Patrick MacGregor in 1781. It is well-known that the MacGregors had been proscribed almost continually from 1604, so they probably were adept at defying an additional proscription aimed at Jacobites. Despite all these Highland activities, the clan has no legal recognition and the chief of a clan has no authority beyond that of a private person; but the old tradition still endures and the evils which accompanied the clan system have been forgotten in the pleasures of such functions as Highland Games, ceilidhs, and marches of pipe bands.

It is only with a great effort that anyone today can realise the conditions of life in Scotland two centuries ago, when the restrictions on Highland activities were lifted. How much more difficult is it, even impossible, for the imagination to take one back to any time in the middle ages when the story of the clans begins.

2. Early History of British Celts.

There are many people who are completely sceptical about the remote Scottish past and take the easiest way out of the situation by refusing to believe anything they read or hear about it. They have, unfortunately, some substantial grounds for the suspension of belief because of the legends and monastic fables which long passed as history. Many of the Scottish 'historians' of early modern times, notably Boece, Fordun and the very learned Buchanan, wrote fabulous histories exalting the Scottish nation at the expense of England and the powerful nations of Europe. They invented lists of Scottish monarchs as far back as the Flood, without any documented foundation. Buchanan was so illustrious in other respects, and his Latinity so splendid, that none of his successors dared question his myths. Some of these fables are still floating around in Hume Brown and even in some modern books whose authors do not care to verify their sources. This state of affairs is quite inexcusable in historians, even of the 19th century, for the Annals and Records of early centuries have been available for reference and comparison since the end of the 18th century. Historians have been very active in the last twenty years and this initiative, collated with archaeology, is intensifying. Yet, as has been happily said, it is easy to get false history into the schools, especially when it flatters the readers, but it seems impossible to get it out. As an example there are many Scots who treat as even holier than Scripture the story that St. Columba was the first missionary to the Picts. They also believe that Gaelic was universally spoken in Scotland at that time and even when given the best authority for the fact that Columba required interpreters to address the Picts, they are still not convinced.

To come now to the true history of the Clan Gregor. As I wrote in my Apology, Joseph Anderson did not believe that it had ever been written, though the raw material was available. I think he was referring more to the terrible times of the persecution and attempted extermination, which were of course adequately documented in enactments and trials, than to the early history of the clan, before their hereditary territories were a prey to feudal acquisitors and they were driven to desperate deeds. It is about this early period that I have taken the greatest trouble to establish the facts, for the obvious reasons that records only exist in a very irregular fashion and many have been carelessly copied or deliberately falsified to suit the purposes of certain religious or political partisans. I am of course indebted for corrections of these early documents to the labours of dedicated students who spent their eyesight and general health in seeking for truth at the bottom of a very muddy historical well. I could never, unaided, have got to it. Still, I had to do a bit of thinking on my own account, and to piece together some imperfect jigsaws. Where I encounter dubious statements, or duplications of names, and other obscurities, I confess failure if I cannot find a solution. I am afraid I have to make several such confessions.

I have spent many more years than I care to remember reading about very early days in Scotland, as well as in other lands: the many incompatible racial elements in Scotland, warring incessantly for a momentary advantage, had no idea of unity until they were ultimately hammered into a sort of cohesion by Edward I. The Celtic peoples were always given to dissension. One could almost say they invented nuclear fission about 500 BC, for no sooner had the nucleus of a colony been set up than it began to fly off from the centre. Had this not been a trait of the British Celts they would have easily resisted the invasions of the Anglo-Saxons, Norse and Danes. In the very early, pre-Roman, days, there were none but Celts in the British Isles, except a few subdued groups of Bronze Age tribes, so the various branches fought one another, rather like the present natives of central New Guinea, who worship the most treacherous warrior, and bring up their infants to study his methods.

The Caledonians, whose numerous tribes were named and their territories defined by early geographers of Mediterranean origin, occupied most of Scotland north of the Forth–Clyde isthmus. This is not news to my readers nor is it news that all the rest of Britain was inhabited by British Celts. Ireland, the home of other Celtic invaders from Europe, was divided between the Gaels or Goidels and the Cruithens, or Irish Picts, who, needless to say, waged war to the knife with one another, with a few brief respites. The Gaels had probably come from Spain and were ambitious, cunning and quarrelsome, probably even more so than the Picts. They crossed the narrow channels into Britain, first in raiding parties known as Scotti to the Romans. When the Romans left, they formed Gaelic colonies in Cornwall, North Wales and S.W. Scotland. But we shall go back in time, momentarily, to study the Caledonians from whose stock may of the later Highland clans, including the MacGregors, were derived.

We are well aware of the tender mercies of the Romans whose common method of execution was crucifixion, but who, under Julius Caesar, massacred and maimed whole nations of Gauls, and carried out the same measures in Britain, exterminating the Iceni who had revolted under Boudicca, or Boadicea, and moving relentlessly north, slaughtering all conditions of people as they came. Finally the remnants of the defiant tribes, headed by the Caledonians under a chieftain whose native name was Latinised to Calgacus, drew to a last stand on what David Macpherson, a veracious and ingenious historian of the 18th century, considered to be Mormond Hill in Buchan, famous as the title of a 'Corn-Kister' ballad. Tacitus, son-in-law of Agricola, was the historian and map-maker of this campaign; naturally he deemed it proper to give his father-in-law his fair share of glory, but, apart from this, his account of the enemy seems to be accurate, if we except the totally fictitious speech which he put into the mouth of Calgacus, whose language Tacitus could not possibly have understood, even if he had heard it. A close reading of Tacitus' lengthy description of the final battle, (where the Romans employed Netherland legions to take the brunt of the hand-to-hand encounter, while the Roman cavalry pursued the fugitives) clearly describes the great plain of Buchan, south-west of 'Taixalorum Promentarium', or Kinnaird Head. The whole region was covered by mangled corpses and smoking ruins, and the Romans and their auxiliaries marched south to winter in Fife, 'in the confines of the Horestii'.

History repeats itself, which proves Hegel's saying to have some truth in it, after all. Edward Bruce, over a thousand years after Agricola, repeated this atrocious massacre in the 'Harrying of Buchan', wherein he destroyed the power of the Comyns, his brother's enemies. But if we wish to leave the savagery of ancient and mediaeval times far behind us, hoping that the advance of Christianity and civilisation will have obliterated these horrific memories, what do we find? Richard Rolt, author of *The Conduct of the Powers of Europe*, who was a contemporary of the Duke of Cumberland, writes this of the behaviour of that noble scion,

> 'The Duke of Cumberland issued a proclamation for disarming such of the clans as refused to surrender themselves; a camp was established at Fort Augustus, whence several detachments were sent to ruin and

depopulate the rebellious country; where the devastation was so great, that, for the space of fifty miles, neither house, man, nor beast was to be seen; which was the entire subjugation of this fierce and intractable people, whom neither the Romans nor Saxons could reduce, and who had often bid defiance to their native kings.'

The region so devastated was not the plain of Buchan, but the people who were so atrociously butchered were descendants of those who had stood up to Agricola at Mons Grampius.

As I shall try to show later, the character of the Caledonians was unchanged for eighteen centuries, for it must not be supposed that the warlike and numerous Clan Gregor and associated clans suddenly arose in some strange manner with no ancestral basis, or without a genetic reservoir from which to draw the peculiar permutations which kept up a steady stream of remarkable individuals. I am not going to seek this reservoir among the Hamitic nomads of the Sahara or the Finnish tribes of the tundra, though, as blood-tests have shown, the Hamitic Berbers of North Africa are identical in blood groups to the Celts of Scotland, Wales and Ireland. But I feel justified in following the fortunes, or misfortunes, of those Caledonians whom the Romans, more than once, drove temporarily beyond Glen More, but who took every opportunity to drive the Romans and their European, Asian, African and British legions south of the Antonine and Hadrian's Walls. Many clans, besides the MacGregors, MacNabs, MacKinnons, MacNishes, and MacPhees were of similar character to the ancient Caledonoi, or Dicaledonoi, but, as I shall demonstrate beyond a peradventure, Rolt's description of their intractability is most applicable to Clan Gregor, for the indisputable reason that none of the other clans was so severely put to the test. The fact that it was probably the over-reaction of the MacGregors to their antagonists that drew upon them the extreme wrath of the powers of state and their encroaching landowners, does not weaken their claim to be direct descendants of the forces that stood in no awe of Caesar.

3. 18th Century MacGregors' Bad Name.

For the time being, I shall pass over that lengthy period, from the end of Roman Britain about 400 AD to the end of Celtic political power in 1746, at Culloden, all of which forms the background for the main body of my history. I would now like to make comments on the reputation which the MacGregors found to be their only inheritance from the past, once they had been very grudgingly and tardily received back, by legal and regal sanction, into the body of the British nation.

This reputation was not enviable, and for long their past activities were regarded as atrocious. Before and after their name was restored to them, it was regarded more as a term of abuse than as an honourable distinction. In the trial of Sir James Stewart, Provost of Edinburgh, for treason in connection with the execution of Montrose, the Lord Advocate, Sir George MacKenzie, 'Bloody MacKenzie', roundly accused Stewart in these terms: 'You are no Stewart. You are just a bare-arsed MacGregor.' No doubt this opprobrious expression was quite commonly applied to them for a long time when sanctioned by such a notable precedent.

Even in England, where ignorance of Scottish history is almost a virtue, the MacGregors were regarded, towards the end of their long outlawing, as an exceptionally wicked and violent people.

To brand an entire clan with such an evil repute, as if they were beasts of prey, untameable and irredeemable, shows a massive prejudice against them. But, even as late as the end of the 18th century, such prejudices were common, and were not confined to recriminations against the MacGregors. David Hume, the most eminent philosopher of his age, a man of very equable judgement, wrote that the negro race were not endowed with the capacity to compete with Europeans in the fields of invention and ingenuity. The authors of the American Declaration of Independence, who were to a great extent men of integrity and political wisdom, spoke in that Declaration, of the American Indians as a completely merciless and bloodthirsty race deserving in turn of no mercy. They made no attempt to differentiate the tribes, to contrast the Seneca with the Apaches, or to recollect that the confederacy of the Five Nations, who occupied territory on the Great Lakes, were peacefully employed in fishing and agriculture for centuries before they were abused by the encroaching white men. The cause of the American Indians' savage reaction, the policy of land-stealing and persecution to the death, was substantially similar to that which led to the MacGregors' violence and bloodshed. But the white Americans naturally did not mention, in such a high-toned document, that their land-grabbing and other aggression was responsible for the growth of a body of irresponsible savages, whom the British were accused of inciting to attack the white settlers.

It is instructive to contrast the above reputation that the MacGregors had, with the opinion of them held by the people who had every reason to know their true character. I mean the Highland clans who were their neighbours. Among the Celts certain pronounced characteristics were, from time immemorial, attached to specific clans, and embodied in proverbial sayings. One of these sayings described three impossible phenomena. 'MacGillEathain gun bhòsd, Domhnullach gun seòltachd, Caimbeulach gun mhòrchuis.' A MacLean without boasting, a MacDonald without cunning, a Campbell without arrogance.

A well-known prayer was

> From the pride of the Grahams,
> From the greed of the Campbells,
> From the wind of the Murrays,
> From the anger of the Drummonds,
> The Good Lord deliver us, Amen.

These were far from complimentary and may have been inspired by clan rivalry, but they had a broad basis of experience to support them. Yet the sayings about the MacGregors were complimentary, and there seems to have been no reproach about their vehemence. In a Gaelic poem by Ian Lom MacDonald, addressed in honour of MacKinnon of Strath (in Skye), the MacGregors (related to MacKinnons) were described as his faithful allies and as 'Clan Gregor of the pipes and the routs', referring to their skill in piping and their ferocity and impetuosity in onslaught. An ancient proverb says of them and of their kinsfolk, the MacNabs: '*Cha robh sgonn-bhalach riamh de chloinn-Ghriogair no brèineag de chloinn an Aba.*' There was never a clown of Clan Gregor, nor a slut of the MacNabs.

It was only outside the Highlands, among the Sassenach, which included the Lowland Scots, that the MacGregors had a reputation for wickedness. In America, where a number of MacGregors emigrated, after taking the Blood Oath not to rebel against King George, they were always regarded as upright and honourable people. In Cape Fear Valley they paid very dearly for making their word their bond, for they lost their lives at the hands of the American rebel forces. The MacGregors had a tendency to over-react and to pay back a debt with compound interest. As has been said of the Hebraic people, 'they were just human, only more so.' A French humorist, in the 19th century, published a volume entitled *La Menagerie*, in which there is an illustration of a caged animal, with the notice, 'This animal is very mischievous, when attacked it defends itself.' Such a notice could have been prominently nailed to the trees long ago in the Balquhidder area.

Dr Johnson, uncrowned king of English society, had a kind of love-hate relationship with the Scots, but, characteristically, even though possessed of 'sheer ignorance' about the MacGregors, he bluntly cast obloquy upon them all. In *Lives of the Poets*, 1781, in his essay on the poet David Mallet, he writes, 'He was by his original, one of the MacGregors, a clan that became about sixty years ago, under the conduct of Robin Roy, so formidable and so infamous for violence and robbery, that the name was annulled by a legal abolition, and when they were all to denominate themselves anew, the father, I suppose, of this author, called himself Malloch.' Johnson did not give the reason for this second change of name to Mallet, but he probably knew that Malloch's enemies, which included all the London Scots, had nicknamed him 'Moloch', for, they alleged, he was prepared to sacrifice anyone for filthy lucre. There is, unfortunately for the good name of the clan, a lot of truth in this accusation, for it was Malloch who, in 1757, wrote a public letter, over the pseudonym 'Plain Man', accusing Admiral Byng of cowardice and bungling; this letter brought to a head the general public discontent over discrimination in favour of high-ranking officers, and roused the rabble to such an extent that poor Byng was executed to appease them. This gave rise to the satirical comment by Voltaire, 'In England it is thought well to kill an admiral from time to time to encourage the others.' Mallet was awarded a life-pension by Lord North, 'For political services', but whether for his attack on Byng, or for his collaboration with James Thomson in composing 'Rule Britannia', I cannot say. He was a genius but his character is equivocal. Johnson in all likelihood was not encouraged by Mallet's behaviour to love the MacGregors, which was unlucky for the MacGregors, for Johnson's influence was far-reaching.

4. Sir Walter Scott to the Rescue.

It was Sir Walter Scott, the succeeding literary giant of Britain, who vindicated the Clan Gregor. He was professionally well-informed about the legal acts dealing with the clan, and, moreover, he had personal contacts with people who still remembered Rob Roy. It should be remembered too that, during Scott's early boyhood, the MacGregors were still under nominal proscription. Rob's eldest son Ranald, or Ronald, still survived at Balquhidder until 1786, about which time Scott, as an apprentice lawyer, had occasion to visit the area and to hear of Rob Roy at first hand. It was not until 1818 that the novel *Rob Roy* was published. In the same year the Rev. Mr. MacLeay brought out a popular collection of tales about Rob Roy. In this coincidental way Rob Roy was brought to the notice of the two main strata of Scottish, and, to a lesser extent, of British society; for those who could not aspire to buy one of the Waverley Novels could afford MacLeay's humbler and more intelligible book. In Cockburnspath public library, over thirty years ago, I chanced upon a copy of MacLeay's book, every page stained crimson through having been thumbed over, perhaps during the midday break, by the field-workers fresh from the red soil of the district. No more sincere testimony could be brought to support Rob Roy's popular appeal. Wordsworth, visiting Glen Gyle and Loch Katrine, (which the latest English TV commentator pronounces Lock Katreen!) wrote the poem 'Rob Roy's Grave' in 1803, under the mistaken belief that Rob was buried near his birthplace, though he was interred in Balquhidder. Wordsworth was one of the first Englishmen to give Rob Roy credit for his chivalrous deeds, and compared him with the English Robin Hood, 'who robbed the rich to pay the poor', but whose actual existence in flesh and blood has never been established, though Joseph Ritson and other researchers, who were no fools, found proof that he was a real person of the name of Robin Fitzooth. It seems almost incredible that last year an English guide to a bus tour in the Trossachs, after telling about Rob's associations, added, 'If there ever was such a man as Rob Roy.'

Almost overnight, in 1818, the MacGregors awoke, like Lord Byron (whose 'Childe Harold' was completed that year), 'to find themselves famous.' R. L. Stevenson pronounced *Rob Roy* to be the best of Scott's works, which would not have been achieved unless Scott had been in complete sympathy with the MacGregors. Scott's own ancestors, the Scotts of Harden, had been stark moss-troopers, every bit as lawless and subject to legislation as the MacGregors, though they did not achieve the distinction of proscription. Several Border clans, e.g. the Grahams, were, however, banished overseas, as were many of the more notorious MacGregors such as Robert Aberach. But most of them came back to their old haunts.

The most popular theatre show for many years was the dramatised version of *Rob Roy*, which on rare occasions, as in 1925, when I saw it, played to packed houses. It seems that the ancient shame attached to the name MacGregor was replaced, in or about 1818, by the glory, and there was a rush, now that the danger and disgrace had been dissipated, to resume the ancient proscribed name.

Some years ago, one of my MacGregor friends, in the Clan Gregor Social Club in Edinburgh, proposed that a Scott Supper should be held annually on August 15th, his birthday, because of his great labours in restoring the good name of the clan. We did not do anything about it at the time, but I still think such a celebration long overdue. We could than have a Burns Supper in mid-winter and a Scott Supper in the Lammas-tide when we often get 'Glorious' weather about the 12th. It is not surprising to know that both Sir John Murray (who became the chief soon after the Proscription was lifted) and his son, Sir Ewan Murray MacGregor, founder of the Clan Gregor Society, and an ancestor of the present Chief Sir Gregor MacGregor, were friends of Sir Walter Scott.

In the third part of this history I shall be due to pay much more attention to Rob Roy and his family, bringing forward some facts which, although long authenticated, have been obscured until now. The more detailed account of the notoriety and infamous end of two of Rob's sons, which arguably was undeserved, left such a bad impression that Scott's vindication of the clan as a whole was undoubtedly made more difficult, and there are still people who malign the MacGregors on false reports that have been long quashed by facts. I am still hopeful of nailing these old lies.

Part 1. Origins.

Chapter 1. Finding Alpin

If my reader cares to ask any Scot, whether a Highlander or Lowlander, a MacGregor, or of any other clan, about the origin of the Clan Gregor, the answer will probably convince the questioner that the whole business is so confused and obscure, and of so little relevance to everyday life, that the sensible thing seems to be to dismiss the problem as insoluble. Most writers on the subject have confined themselves to the traditions hallowed by Sir Walter Scott and others. The MacGregors themselves seem to have been content to believe vaguely in the regal origin of the clan, as it is embodied in the Gaelic motto *''S Rìoghail mo Dhrèam'*, 'My lineage is Royal'. Of this belief in royal origin Scott says, in the notes on *Rob Roy*, that the 'clan claimed descent from Gregor, third son of King Alpin who flourished in 787 AD.' Miss A. G. M. MacGregor, in the first volume of her *History of Clan Gregor* published about 1900, repeats the above claim in her title-page. It is also repeated by John MacGregor W.S. in the summary of his years of research on the MacGregor records in the Register House in Edinburgh. He says that all writers on the subject seem to concur in this finding. After a very long search in all the ancient annals of kings of early mediaeval Scotland, and in parallel chronicles as noted by students of repute, I can find no historical basis for the above statements. But Miss MacGregor, in her massive history, does adduce evidence that Gregor was not Alpin's son.

There is a phrase in Isaac Watt's great hymn,

> 'Time like an ever-rolling stream
> Bears all its sons away;'

which applies even to kings, and particularly to the very transient rulers of the Picts and Scots, however important they may have imagined themselves to be. Some of these very minor monarchs have been blown up to ridiculous proportions by their fabulists. J. H. Burton, historian, gives a sarcastic account of one such claim, which concerns a 'king' of the Scots of Dalriada, named Eochaidh, Hugh, or Achaius, to whom I refer shortly in my search for Alpin. Burton, quoting Boece, the fabulist, says that Charlemagne, Emperor of most of Europe, entered into a league with Achaius, to supply the Empire with learned men to teach in the universities. When we come to look closer at this mighty peer of Charlemagne, we find that, far from ruling over Dalriada, roughly Argyllshire, he was holding on to Kintyre, his presence tolerated there by Donald MacConstantine, Pictish lieutenant-governor of Dalriada. Charlemagne had almost certainly never heard of him. Although we do not judge the character of men by their worldly circumstances and cannot fully support Burton when he speaks of Achaius, 'living in a sort of kraal built of mud and wattles', this example should prevent us from taking kings, either the Scots or the Picts, at the exaggerated estimation of early Scots historians.

I now return to the particular individuals whom many writers agree were the originators of Clan Gregor, 'Alpin and his third son, Gregor.' Alpin was a common Pictish name meaning son of the hills, or of the hilly island. There were three kings, at least, known to history as Alpin, and perhaps sub-kings also, not now remembered. The son of King Nechtan was also Alpin, but, although he was not likely, under Pictish rule of succession, to have succeeded his father, he was slain in battle in 693, so is eliminated. All the Alpin kings were Picts, however mixed they may have been in their ancestry, for the description 'Pict' in the age of the Alpins has to be qualified by saying that there was a great deal of intermarriage between the Picts and Scots, Britons and Irish (both Gaels and Cruithens), so that the dividing line of nationality is indeterminable. The name Alpin is variously spelt Alpine, Elphin, Ailphin. I spell it consistently Alpin, and, where their surname is the same, I add the father's byname.

In order of time the first king Alpin was Alpin Mac Eachaidh (the genitive, in Gaelic, of Eochaidh or Hugh). He reigned over the Picts from 726 to 728. Perhaps because he was only a half-Pict (his father Hugh having borne a favourite Scotic name) he had already reigned over the Dalriadic Scots for a short time. If only to show that there still remains some knowledge of these remote, and obscure monarchs, allow me to give a few salient details of his career.

According to Isabel Henderson, in her study *The Picts*, he was one of four Pictish contestants for the throne of Pictavia, in the short bitter Civil War, which ended in 729 with the supremacy of Angus I and the crushing of the others. Alpin, with the survivors of his army, was expelled from Pictavia by Angus, but he hovered about the southern borders, descending alike on Britons of Strathclyde, Angles of Lothian and Dumfries, and Picts of Galloway, to rob and pillage. He is said to have been King of Strathclyde for a time. In the great battle of Catoc or Maes-y-dawc, whose field has been forgotten, Alpin took part with all his forces. In this conflict the apparently invincible Angus was, strangely enough, aided by the forces of Eadbert, king of Mercia. Against them were the armies of the Britons of Strathclyde, aided by Alpin and the Dalriads. It was, like Leipsic, a 'Battle of Nations', quite forgotten now. Angus and Eadbert won, and Alpin was shortly afterwards slain near Loch Ryan in an ambush. His son Bili had died (the Strathclyde annals say) in 722, so this is not the Alpin we want. But we are getting nearer our goal for this Alpin, slain after Catoc in 750, was the grand-uncle of the more famous, or infamous, Alpin of the following century, of whom also only a few details, and those not all creditable, are recorded.

Before we come to him, however, we ought to mention the intermediate Alpin, king of the Picts, Alpin MacWroid, MacUuroid, or MacFeroid, who reigned from 775 to 780. He comes nearest in time to the traditional Alpin, though he is not yet the wanted man. I draw him into my net because of his importance in the forthcoming argument about regal succession. I would like however to make a small digression about his father's name and to explain how Wroid can be pronounced Feroid. This was a Pictish peculiarity of pronunciation which lasts to this day in Buchan, to prove that the Picts as a people persisted there, despite their changes of language. Words like 'who' and 'what' are still pronounced 'fa' and 'fat', and Wroid in South Pictland was Feroid in North Pictland. He had only one daughter known to history, who married a Scotic king named Hugh, and named her first-born after her father, Alpin. Here then is the third man, who seems to fit our case, for his son Kenneth based his claim to the Pictish throne on the fact that his grandmother was of Pictish royal blood. The Picts, like most of the British, as well as the Irish Cruithens, put more emphasis on female ancestry than on paternity, though they did not allow a queen to rule over them as did the Iceni and Brigantes of Britain, whose queens were also demi-goddesses. The 'practical Picts', as Robert Chambers calls them, realised that a boy's best friend was his mother, and his father sometimes only a very fitful factor.

This third and last Alpin, like his grand-uncle, was also named Alpin MacHugh, but, to distinguish him from his earlier relative, he is named, in Gaelic, Alpin Mac Eachaidh Anguibh; in Latin, Alpinus filius Eochal (or Achaius) Venenosi; in English, Alpin, son of Hugh the Poisonous. How Hugh got this insalubrious title we are not told, but all records, even of the Scots, give him this description, which is by no means figurative, for these bynames of kings were always based on fact. Ritson, the historian, says 'he was, notoriously, King of the Scots.' His son Alpin reigned in Dalriada from 834 to 837. He then made an attempt to rule over the Picts, which, by Pictish law, he was quite entitled to do as his mother was a Pictish princess. But he chose what, for his own interest, seemed a very opportune time, but what, from every moral standard, was inexcusable. The Picts under Angus II had just suffered what has been called the 'Flodden of the Picts', losing their King and most of their leaders and warriors in a defeat by the heathen Norse. Angus II's young son was trying to gather his scattered forces, when Alpin, a fellow-Christian, attacked him on Easter Day, 837. As Easter was the only important Christian anniversary at that time, it was observed with awesome solemnity. The fixing of the Easter date, which was traditionally related to the full moon following the spring equinox, was for long the cause of dissension amongst different sects. One rather ridiculous incident, due to this difference, was about an Anglian king and queen of opposite views on Easter, who consequently celebrated Lent at different times, and may have given rise to the rhyme, 'Jack Sprat could eat no fat, his wife could eat no lean.' At any rate, Alpin's attack on Easter Day was an unpardonable sin. He did not long survive to enjoy his triumph. In the autumn of that year he was defeated by a reconstituted Pictish army, and beheaded in a ceremony of retribution. Beheadal was the most shameful of deaths, in Pictish ethics. Drowning was the usual fate reserved for unwanted kings. Without going into gory details, the Picts, rough and ready though they were, compared very favourably with later barbarians, who excelled themselves in refined humiliation by drawing, quartering, and burning genitals under the still quivering noses of their political and religious opponents. Even as late as 1820 a poor natural, James Wilson, was beheaded (after being hanged) on Glasgow Green, for leading a protest march against starvation. The Picts appear almost benign in this lurid light.

Regarding the end of Alpin MacEachaidh Anguibh, the Nomina Regum, or List of Kings states:

DCCCXXXVII. Hic (Alpinus) occisus est in Gallewathia postquam eam penitus destruxit et devastavit.

837. He (Alpin) was slain in Galloway after he had utterly destroyed and wasted it.

Such is the confusion, however, among these old records that is quite possible that this Alpin, in the circumstances of his death, is being mistaken for his grand-uncle of the same name, who also was killed in Galloway and who had also devastated it. But the earlier Alpin is recorded as being slain by a single ambusher at a ford, while the later Alpin was prominently executed, after his defeat and capture, before a large army.

One would suspect that a very unfriendly pen had given this account of Alpin, whom the Clan Gregor have for so long seemed so anxious to claim as father of their founder Gregor. The chronicler of this account was the 13th-century Henry of Huntingdon, who had access to manuscripts, contemporary to Alpin's period, which have long since perished. Although Henry had no axe to grind, this does not mean that the originals from which he wrote were unprejudiced. Still, Henry does not make any moral reflections on Alpin, of the vituperous sort that an Anglian chronicler made upon the worthy King Nechtan because of a religious difference, so it may be assumed that Alpin's history was only a little below the standard of an early mediaeval monarch of Scotland, or any other European country in Christendom, who, for his own advantage, went behind the backs of his own people when they were engaged in a life and death struggle with the Gentiles, or heathen Norse and Danes.

Isabel Henderson remarks that in this account is the only hint that Alpin's older son Kenneth may have been provoked, by the manner of his father's death, to carry on his campaign against his executioners. It seems unnatural to me that he should not have exerted himself to the utmost, to avenge his father Alpin, despite all the latter's moral obliquities.

Chapter 2. Age of Anarchy.

It was an age of anarchy in Scotland. Where, for three centuries previously, the records had been carefully kept, we are now thrown back on conjecture, to a large extent. Most of the records were destroyed in the sacking of the monasteries by the Norse. What remained were further diminished by the depredations of Edward I, in his attempts to master the alien traditions of the Scots; then came the destruction of the monasteries and abbeys, in the fury of the Reformations; Cromwell completed the vandalism unwittingly, by returning the purloined records on board ship, and having them nearly all lost by shipwreck. It is a miracle that even a few scraps remain to us, mostly transcribed from the originals, to enable us to make a blurred picture of Picts ruling Scots (under Constantine) and Scots ruling Picts intermittently. One thing appears certain. The Pictish power is waning from Fife to Shetland under the constant Norse attrition; so is the Scotic power under the same attacks down the Hebridean seas. In 806 the Vikings sacked Iona and martyred many Columban monks. In 849, after several such assaults the Abbot took Columba's relics to Ireland, and Iona was left derelict. Before this year the Scots became desperate to seek safety inland to the east. To avoid destruction they must at all costs, either by peaceful means or by force, amalgamate with the Picts. Desperate diseases need desperate remedies, and this is the only excuse one can offer for the behaviour of either of the Alpin MacHughs, great-uncle or grand-nephew, or for their successor Kenneth MacAlpin.

My reader may very well remark that there was little to choose between any mediaeval warriors. They were all forced by circumstances to be treacherous scoundrels. An anthropologist has recently surmised that the early hominids, our respected fathers that begat us, owed their success in the survival race to that great deterrent, the club, with which they dashed out the brains, such as they were, of their rivals the baboons. Our mediaeval ancestors of the 'Heroic Age' certainly reverted to type, a danger still with us. In Welsh accounts, not romanticised, but straight, King, or war-leader, Arthur is portrayed as a cuckold with the temper of a distraught bear, not at all the model for a Tennysonian gentleman; Lancelot is an unprincipled womaniser; Guinevere, the adulterous queen, sleeps around with as many of the Knights of the Round Table as can spare a short time from rescuing dragons from unfair ladies.

No early king of Scotland, whether a half-Pict named MacAlpin, or MacBeth, or a seven-eighths Pict with the pre-Celtic name of Canatulachama, Bliesblituth, Erp or Usconbuts, specially deserves the name of usurper. They were nearly all usurpers; it was common practice for the slayer of a monarch to assume his victim's crown. It was to obviate this violence that the Scots agreed to abide by the law of Tanistry, or male succession, and the Picts to elect kings from the maternal side, by the consensus of seven sub-kings.

It would have been much better for Scotland, and, after 1603, for England also, had the Pictish method of electing kings been retained. The Scottish monarchs from Robert I to James VI, attempted, despite failures of the male line, to follow the ancient Dalriadic custom. They suffered all the disasters that minority and female succession (The Monstrous Regiment or Regimen of Women) invited, with resultant civil wars and general misery. The preposterous principle of Divine Right emanated from this belief in the infallibility of inherited genius. The Picts were too shrewd to swallow that attractive bait, and in this way alone, if in no other, they showed that their political ability was superior to any system that succeeded their loss of sovereignty. So all this millennium of misrule was the result of Viking disruption.

The MacGregors must be very hard up for a royal origin if they persist in claiming descent from Alpin; that is to say, if they want a respectable prototype. Morally, he was just a jet-black pot amongst a lot of soot-black kettles, all jealous of him and jangling about to push him off the hob. Only one king of the Picts at that time seems to have, temporarily, got sick of the rat-race; this was Nechtan, a religious man, who had persuaded his churchmen, who were under his ecclesiastic authority, to adopt the Roman tonsure and Eastertide, and who had expelled any Columban monks who refused to conform. He joined a monastery, but kept on interfering in politics from his holy fox-hole, eventually emerging at the head of his followers to back up Alpin MacHugh (the Non-poisonous), a claimant to the Pictish throne. Nechtan should have kept to his cell. After Alpin's flight, Nechtan reigned a month or two, was defeated by Angus I, then died of a broken heart, due either to disappointment or a dirk.

The royal predecessor of Alpin MacWroid was Kenneth who, it appears from the records, left his troubles rather abruptly. It would be interesting to know more details but the chronicler records picturesquely and laconically, '*ex voragine hujus coenulentis vitae eripitur*' (he was snatched out of the whirlpool of this tumultuous life). *Coenulentis* is untranslatable and is meant to describe the appearance of a snake-pit, or swarm of cockroaches, fighting for advantage.

I think on that delicate note I shall leave my reader to imagine what a miserable, brutal and short existence was the fate of most people born into the time of the Alpins. Luckily there is a ray of hope for us MacGregors, trying to find a royal connection of some value. We have still to unravel the mystery of Gregor. And here the plot, thick enough before, becomes practically opaque, but with patience and perseverance we shall see light in the end.

Kenneth MacAlpin was the first king of the united Picts and Scots. As we have seen, it was 'unite or perish'. In 843 he assumed the throne of Pictavia. The Pictish capital then was at Scone. At other times Abernethy, Forteviot and Inverness were the chief seats. Some of the annals say he began to reign as late as 850, but this is not supported by a consensus. He was either crowned upon the sacred inaugural stone seat of the Picts (as Sir Thomas Innes, the Lord Lyon, contended), or else he placed his foot upon it after the Scotic style. As he did not bring the Scotic Stone of Destiny to Scone from Dunstaffnage until 850, that may account for the report that his proper coronation took place then. He certainly did not use the Lia Fal, or 'Stone of Bethel', carried, tradition says, from the Holy Land, for, all through the 9th and 10th centuries, at least, it remained at the old Irish capital of Tara. In any case, according to the latest students of Irish history and Celtic tradition, the Lia Fal was a phallic symbol which sang out when the proper candidate for high kingship approached it. He had also to pass several exacting tests to prove his worthiness. The Lia Fal had nothing to do with Jacob; obviously this addition was a monastic myth propagated when the heathen customs were superseded.

Kenneth MacAlpin's reason for being crowned, (probably with a plain circlet of gold, in the Pictish tradition), was perhaps because he wished to insist on his Pictish sympathies and get the Pictish people to accept him. The old tale that he destroyed the Picts is self-evidently nonsense. He is said to have treacherously invited the Pictish sub-kings to a feast and assassinated them by leading them onto a covered pit planted with upturned spikes. But the Picts did not easily accept his 'shotgun wedding' arrangements with the Scots. In the Pictish Chronicles we read that, in 842–3, a Pictish regional king, probably of Fortrenn (Strathearn and Fife) went to war with Kenneth to prevent his taking over Pictavia. This King Wroid and his sons Brude, Drust, and Kenneth, each attempted to take the throne but were defeated and slain by MacAlpin. Even after his coronation he had a struggle to maintain his kingdom. Much of his life is shrouded in mystery but some things are authenticated. He died about 858, the fatal disease being *tumore ani*, an uncomfortable end. According to Scotic custom he was carried to Iona, which was abandoned then, but, the Vikings not being about he was buried there with the Dalriadic Kings. As the Tanist, or male successor, his brother Donald succeeded and reigned four years.

Chapter 3. Gregor Breaks in.

On Donald MacAlpin's death, another of Alpin's sons should have succeeded, for Kenneth had died prematurely and Donald was not senile either, for he is described in Gaelic, in the Chronica Regum and other records, as '*Dhomhnaill dhreachruaid*' or Donald of the ruddy countenance. Another MacAlpin, named Hugh, presumably one of Kenneth's brothers, named after Hugh (the Poisonous), died in 940, according to the Annals of the Scots, at the age of over a hundred, for Alpin was executed in 837. Why was he not allowed to succeed Donald? In 862 he would be a young man about thirty, quite a suitable candidate. Where, too, was

Gregor, the alleged 'third son of Alpin'? He does not come forward either, and the throne is mounted by Constantine MacKenneth, who rules for fourteen years before meeting catastrophe at the hands of the Gentiles (Vikings). In a great battle at Inverdovet, a hamlet near Newport, Fife, he was slain with most of his army. Kenneth's younger son, Hugh MacKenneth, then took over but lasted barely a year. He was slain in Glen Artney, far inland, so the sea-rovers are exonerated. Indeed, the Pictish Chronicle states baldly, '*Ed Mac Kinet uno anno. Interfectus in bello in Strathalin (Strathalum) a Girg filio Dungal.*' (Hugh MacKenneth for one year. Slain in war in Strathearn (?) by Gregor MacDungal). He was buried in Iona. Such was the short uneventful reign of 'Fairhaired' or 'Swift-footed' Hugh (the Gaelic record says the first, and the Latin the second; perhaps he was both).

Now Gregor, at last, enters the page of history, his hands blood-stained. If we are to believe the tradition, supported by Scott and others, the blood is that of his own nephew. This would have been typical of mediaeval monarchs. Malcolm (Canmore) III 'causid one of his brothers to be behedid and put out the eyes of another brother and kept him in Gedworth-castel yn prison, fering lest they should put him from his kingdom.' Solomon, that paragon of kings, slew his brother Adonijah and his cousin Joab.

But Gregor, according to several reliable historical sources, was no relation of Hugh the Fair, nor of Constantine, of Kenneth, nor of Alpin, His father was Dungal, a Pict, or perhaps a half-Pict, of Fortrenn. There is just a shade of suspicion that Dungal may have been a son of Hugh the Poisonous and consequently a grand-uncle of Hugh Mac-Kenneth. But Dungal was a fairly common name, so this remote relationship cannot be proved, and Gregor may not have slain a close relation.

The Scots having been nearly annihilated at Inverdovet, they were not in a strong position. Indeed the tables were turned on them, and the Picts were able to insist on a successor to Hugh MacKenneth, in the person of Gregor MacDungal. On comparing six contemporary chronicles, or their later transcriptions, we can clearly see how it was possible for history to be falsified, by omissions of facts that were repugnant to certain political or ecclesiastical parties. The Nomina Regum (List of Kings), The Chronica Regum, the Chronicles of Melrose, the Chronicles of Elegies and the Chronicles of the Picts make no mention at all of Hugh Mac-Run, a grandson of Kenneth through Kenneth's daughter, wife of Run of Strathclyde, who is alleged in the Chronicles of the Scots to have reigned over the Picts and Scots for eleven years. But the first four of the above speak of Grig Mac-Dunegal or Gregor MacDungal, of his civic and military achievements, of his deposal and death, and of the unusual circumstances of this strange event. The Annals of the Scots report an alternative statement in these terms, 'Others say that Kenneth's son Grig reigned here for that he was foster-father and manager (tutor) to Hugh (MacRun).'

Here is confusion worse confounded, if, against all the run of evidence, we credit this hearsay. Gregor is described by the Scots, obviously in their anxiety to keep the throne in the family, as a son of Kenneth. As two of Kenneth's sons had already reigned and been slain, Gregor is made out to be a third son, contrary to all the other contemporary records. But even the hearsay of the Chronicles of the Scots does not claim him as a third son of Alpin, so how this myth was allowed to run so long is a poor reflection on the historians of Clan Gregor.

Gregor's prominence was apparent to all in his comparatively long reign from 878 to 889. If he reigned conjointly with Hugh MacRun, Kenneth's grandson, there is little mention of his sleeping partner. The Scotic party tried their best to minimise his deeds and influence. That is understandable, because he had broken into the dynasty of Kenneth MacAlpin. But what is not comprehensible, if historians live up to their first qualification of being objective, is why this attempted obliteration of eleven years of an authenticated Scottish monarch should still persist to the present day. An obvious answer to this very disturbing question, which affects the integrity of Scottish historians, is that Gregor is a stumbling block to all those who are thirled to the belief that the Picts were destroyed by Kenneth MacAlpin. This is a fable which forms only a very small part of what Miss Mitchison, recently writing in the *Times Literary Supplement*, labelled 'the historical garbage of Scotland', that has long passed for truth. I should like in some other place to collect this garbage under the title of a parody beginning 'In the Garbage of Old Gaul, with the Liars of Old Rome'. Luckily, Professor Barrow, with ample documentary proof, is at present overturning much of this false imagery. I hope that he may convert other historians of Scotland to an objective persuasion, for in a recent book on the subject, one of our professors, whom I forbear to name, had apparently never heard of Gregor MacDungal, (entitled, the Great, by the Scotic Church), and ridiculed the MacGregors for their ignorance in claiming descent from *Pope* Gregory the Great, seventh of that illustrious name. Even Isabel Henderson does not mention Gregor by name in her comprehensive book on the Picts, though one would have thought that such a controversial figure would have at least merited a historian's comment.

Chapter 4. The Last Pictish King.

King Gregor is recorded as a conqueror of 'Anglia'; of course this does not mean England, but is the old name for Tynedale and Lothian. The latter was a province much more extensive than the present region and covered all the south-east of Scotland as far south as the Dumfriesshire Esk. It was racially related to Northumbria. At various times the Picts and Angles had invaded one another's territory, and Gregor's conquest is simply a sign of an upsurge of Pictish military power, backed up by the hot fighting stuff provided by the Dalriadic Scots. Gregor is also said to have been successful in conquests in 'Hibernia', but no specific area is mentioned. In all likelihood he would be supporting the Dalriads of Ulster, who were of the same people as their Argyll tribesmen.

Armies at that time, and for long after, were not known to one another by regular uniforms. The only way to recognise enemies was by their aggressive attitude and alien shouts. The Britons of Wales, for example, named all their enemies Loegrians, because the first invaders were of that people. When the Saxons, and others of Germanic races, took the field centuries later they were called Loegrians. Taliesin, a 6th-century bard, says in 'Death Song for Owain ab Urien', describing the Anglian dead,

> 'Sleepeth the host of wide Loegria
> with sunlight in their eyes.'

The only reference to Gregor's conquest of 'Anglia' is to be found in the Chronicles of Dunelm (Durham) for the year 885, which tell of an innumerable host of Scottish barbarians, who cruelly plundered Lindisfarne and ravaged the surrounding countryside until, by the heavenly intervention of St. Cuthbert, the patron saint of all Anglia, they were swallowed up by an earthquake. This must have been a heavenly intervention indeed, for, in all the historical records of Britain's seismic disturbances, only one life has been lost, and that was of a very unlucky pedestrian in England, (London, I think) who was struck on the head by a falling chimney-pot during an earth-tremor.

From the same Chronicles of Dunelm, however, we are informed that previously, in 883, owing to the cruel inroads of the Vikings or Danes the monks abandoned Lindisfarne and carried off the bones of St. Cuthbert and other precious relics to the high rock of Durham, where they built a fortification which developed later into Durham Cathedral. Seismology has no records for 885, but astronomy has very precise records, and it is known for a mathematical certainty that there was an eclipse of the sun that year about midday on June 16th, the area of totality being across the North of England, Ulster and the Highlands of Scotland. It is quite within the elastic bounds of monkish mythology that the requirements of a suitable miracle, to accompany the transfer of St. Cuthbert's bones to a new resting-place, would easily convert the terror of total eclipse, at noontide in a cloudless midsummer day, into an earthquake to swallow Scots, Picts, Danes or Norse.

As I shall tell shortly, Gregor felt the effects of this total eclipse before very long, through the machinations of ecclesiasts, who so far departed from honesty as to pervert the truth, and used every trick in, or out, of the book to get an advantage for themselves. I could fill the rest of this chapter with mediaeval Scottish miracles alone, from St. Columba's collaboration with the Loch Ness Monster, to the miraculous opening of a box of relics to Bruce before Bannockburn. Europe being a hagiological boneyard in the Middle Ages, all that was needed, to oust the historical St. Riaghuil from Kilrymont, and bring in St. Andrew to head a religious takeover, was a bag of old bones purporting to have come from Patras in Greece, but which probably came from no farther along the coast of Europe than Jarrow in County Durham. Whole skeletons of apostles and saints were shown by the dozen, often in duplicate and triplicate, in many churches in Christendom, none of these bones being any different from a beast that had perished on the gallows. St. Andrew, a humble, genial, self-effacing man, would have been very embarrassed had he known of his future role amongst the arrogant tribes of the Scots and Russians.

In domestic affairs Gregor is best known for his attempt, well before his time, to become the first ecumenical monarch in history, by using his position, as State head of the Pictish Church, to grant equality of status to the Scotic or Columban Church. His motives he kept to himself, but it is obvious that he earnestly wished to win the goodwill of the Scots and unite the nation. However, his beneficent law, equalising the Christian authorities, was not taken in a Christian spirit by his own people, the Picts, and he incurred the well-known '*bilis theologicum*' whose cure does not yet come within medical dictionaries. So bad an attack of bile did the Pictish Churchmen suffer, that, when they got what they interpreted as a sure sign from heaven that Gregor (or Ciricius) was under God's severe displeasure, they could scarcely believe their luck. It chanced that the total eclipse of June 16, 885, fell on the feast-day of St. Ciricius. The birds retired to roost and the stars shone brightly at noon: all the Christians (Columbans, Catholics and Culdees) were scared out of their wits, and looked about for some good reason why God was showing his wrath. The Pictish churchmen soon supplied it. Gregor had been weighed in the balances and found wanting. The gullible as usual were not allowed to see whose thumb was on the scales. It could be asked why the Scotic clergy did not redress the balance, for they did not interfere when Gregor and his young co-ruler were together deposed a year or two later. Although they were grateful to Gregor for his 'gift of liberty' as it is called in their records, on the political side they wished to get rid of him and bring back the dynasty of Kenneth MacAlpin. In fact, they did this, for, on Gregor's death at the hands of his fellow-Picts, probably (though it cannot be verified) at the incitation of the superstitious, in Dundurn, his fortress near Comrie, his throne was occupied by Donald MacConstantine, a grandson of Kenneth, who reigned for eleven years; during which the Norsemen wasted Pictland and finally slew Donald near Forres in Moray. Gregor had been allowed burial in Iona, and apparently all memory of him was buried there also for we look in vain, in any records, for his descendants, though it seems unlikely that he left none.

One of the Kincardineshire parishes dedicated a church and its surrounding parish, either to Gregor, or to the saint after whom he was named; the old name of the church and village was Ecclesia Cirig, corrupted to Ecclescraig. (I have an idea that Selkirk or Selcraig may have once been called Cil-Cirig or church of Gregor.) This is as near to canonisation as Gregor got, but his memory was apparently sufficiently sanctified to denominate a clan, however unholy were some of their later acts.

After Gregor's reign, and probably due to his legislation in the matter of Church authority, the united Kingdom of Picts and Scots seems to have become much more of a reality than the United Kingdom of Scotland and England after 1603. After Gregor's death the name of the kingdom was changed, and the kings' titles, instead of being in Latin form *Rex*

Pictorum', were *'Ri Albain'*, which was intelligible to all, for the Picts, although they probably for a few generations spoke their peculiar form of P-Celtic, gradually were forced, in all sorts of ways, to speak the Q-Celtic or Gaelic. The same kind of change, just as lamentable as it appears to be inevitable, has been overtaking Gaelic for two centuries, so, in a way, the suppression of Pictish language, culture, history and tradition has been avenged by time.

The name Gregor was a common Christian name, in various forms, in every part of Europe and indeed also in Asia and Africa.

Although the memory of Gregor MacDungal was allowed to fade, there was a Gregor, son of Kenneth III, and also a Gregor MacDuff. The first was a regional ruler or sub-king, while the second was a thane of Fife. They could perhaps have been related to the first Gregor, the king. The fact of the name being retained shows that there was no stigma attached to it in the age immediately following him.

Chapter 5. The Pope Raises the Clans

We have now been successful in tracing Gregor from whom the clan Gregor is said to be descended. The next problem is to explain how this Pictish monarch, who uniquely broke into the Scotic line, gave his name to a clan which, as I shall show, was not in existence as Clan Gregor until, at the earliest, well into the eleventh century, two centuries after the death of King Gregor MacDungal and, if there was any relationship with Gregor MacKenneth III, a sub-king, a full century after his time.

According to W. F. Skene, in *Celtic Scotland*, the related clans, MacGregor, MacNab and MacKinnon, originated around the monastic foundation or abthanerie (Gaelic, *abdhaine*, the territory or jurisdiction of an *ab*, or abbot) of Glen Dochart, between Strathearn and Glen Orchy, in Central Perthshire. This region is associated with the early

Irish Pict missionary, St. Fillan, whose name is still embodied in the village of that name. The saint, like most others in those warlike times, made his establishment close under a great fortress, Dundurn, or the Fort on the Earn, which, be it noted, was the scene of King Gregor's activities and death by violence: but that was three centuries after St. Fillan's abship, and two centuries earlier than the rise of the MacGregors, MacNabs and MacKinnons.

For five centuries, then, this picturesque and comparatively fertile mountainous region, capable of supplying all the needs of a numerous population with firing, shelter, weapons, food and drink, was under the guidance of the abthanerie of St. Fillan's successors, either in Strathearn, or in associated monasteries and churches. The people of this extensive area supported the religious establishments, and, in return, were helped both spiritually and materially by the accumulated techniques and wisdom of the abbots. In times of war, which, as I have indicated, became increasingly frequent and severe after the beginning of the eighth century, the religious orders, whose existence was bound up in the whole community, did not scruple to take active part.

W. F. Skene thought that the monastery in Glen Dochart was a Columban foundation, and no doubt it was for its earlier part, but, as the Annals of Ulster, (which are usually reliable) record for the year 717, *'Expulsio familiae Iae trans dorsum Britanniae a Nectano rege'*, the expulsion of the monks of Iona beyond (i.e. west of) Drumalbyn by King Nechtan. Those monks of the Columban order who decided to adopt the tonsure and Easter style of Rome were allowed to remain and carry on with the labours of the ministry.

Two centuries and a half after this banishment, during which period the Pictish Church was in unquestioned control of the whole area, a new situation began to develop. The 'gift of liberty' granted by King Gregor was making the Scotic Church a little impatient to obtain some substantial results of this legislation. They were being excluded from the 'muinntirs', or monasteries, of the Picts by a church law which ordained that the Abbot of these must be a Pict by birth. On the other hand, the Pictish Abbots were aware of the pressure from their rivals, who had already inserted the small end of the wedge by being granted Vicarships in the Pictish Church.

Finghin, (Latin form, Findanus), was the Abbot of Glen Dochart in 966. A man of action, he packed his small necessities in a satchel and set off for Rome to get this question settled at the source. Though a hazardous journey, even centuries later, it was often undertaken by Scots and Picts, Anglo-Saxons and Welsh, in the time of the full authority of the Church, when there were great webs of *'via sanctae'*, or roads of sanctuary, all over Europe, as far north as Scotland. Anyone molesting travellers had to look out for trouble; there was no escape for them in this world, or the next. MacBeth MacFinleg, whom Shakespeare so unwarrantedly traduced, made the journey to Rome in 1050. The Chronicles of Melrose record, *'Rex Scotiae Macbeth ad Romae argentum spargendo distribuit'*, Macbeth the King of Scotland distributed silver at Rome by scattering it about. As Ritson wryly comments, 'The only instance of liberality in a Scottish monarch; very few of Macbeth's successors ever having had any money to distribute.' Canute also went to Rome, and even Dunwallo, the king of Strathclyde, went there and was buried there in 974.

All roads led to Rome in 966 also, and Finghin obtained audience of John XIII, who listened attentively to explanations being given by Finghin (in Latin, the lingua franca, for the Pope on this occasion did not speak Celtic, though several of them did). Finghin's solution to the problem of getting Pictish successors to the Abthanerie in Glen Dochart and elsewhere (for he was also titular Ab of Iona, in this Viking era of destruction) was quite simple. He would provide them himself, if he could get the Papal sanction to marry. This John readily granted. It was not common practice, the clergy being almost wholly celibate, but in the abnormal circumstance this rule was waived.

In this way, arose in time the clan MacFinghin, or MacKinnon, (genitive case) and MacNab (Mac an Aba). Many of the Scottish Highland clans had churchmen as their founders in this era. Such clan names as MacPherson (son of the parson), MacVicar, and perhaps MacAustillan, (son of the Augustinian) bear this out.

But the clan MacGregor appear to be somewhat different for there is no record of an abbot named Gregor or Gregorius, though that is not to deny him existence. We can solve this problem, however, in rather an oblique way, by referring to a document unique in Scottish history, or perhaps in any other history; it is known as the Inquest, or Enquiry, upon the Quigrich or Crozier-head of St. Fillan (an object of rare beauty in Celtic metal-work which may be seen any time in the Museum of Antiquities* in Edinburgh).

On 14th April 1428, John Speirs, Bailie of Glen Dochart, conducted this Inquest on the Quigrich, which was in the hereditary possession of the Dewar family, and was used as authority to pursue and recover stolen property. Three of the signatories were of the Clan Gregor. While the other persons sign, or make a mark, as MacNabs, MacAustillans and MacCallums, the Clan Gregor men sign Donaldus Gregorii etc. signifying by the genitive case of Gregorius and the absence of Mac that they belong to the Gregory group or clan but are not descendants by blood. It might be objected that the Gaelic genitive case was used in surnames, so why not in Latin? It is however the absence of Mac which is significant. Perhaps that is why, to this day, as well as through the centuries of records of their deeds of violence, the MacGregors were generally described as Clan gregoure or some similar spelling.

There is a Gaelic tradition that Finghin was King Gregory's grandson, but tradition often leaps over logical and factual gaps; in this instance, a century. But when Gregory was slain in Dundurn in 889 he was not an aged man for he had recently led warlike expeditions in person. His sons or daughters would be perhaps minors at his death, and their children would not achieve maturity until the middle of the tenth century. Finghin was a middle-aged man of responsible

* This item is now in the National Museum of Scotland, Edinburgh.

position in 966. He could, as far as time goes, claim to be Gregory's grandson, and, for Clan Gregor's tradition of descent, it would be very helpful, but apparently in 1428 the Clan Gregor men were not very sure. Or perhaps there is some other explanation of their peculiar signatures. I would like to know of any.

It occurs to me that this uncertainty may well have arisen because some of the Glen Dochart or Strathearn people were known to be directly descended from Gregor by other grandchildren, perhaps cousins of Finghin who, had they been called upon, might have signed MacGregor. But we have no evidence of these. We must not suppose however, that Finghin existed in a vacuum of population. To support the abthanerie, hundreds of people with different ranks and occupations would be required. What kind of people were they?

To get an adequate answer to this question, which at first sight seems insoluble, if not fatuous, I decided for the moment to leave the annals and records of kings and abbots, and consult the very intensive studies of Dr. Beddoe, the leading British ethnologist of last century, and an acknowledged authority on the very intricate racial composition, not only of Britain but of Europe and beyond. My interest was mainly the very restricted one relating to the Central Highlands of Scotland, especially Perthshire. Dr. Beddoe has some interesting things to say about the Caledonians, to whom I referred in my introduction, but, as many of the clans could claim to be descended from them, I shall confine myself to the area of West Central Perthshire where Finghin and Gregor lived.

Beddoe conducted a very meticulous census of about a hundred people at random over this area, measuring skulls to get an index from each, noting height, eye and hair colour, and other personal characteristics. He published these in his study of *Races of Britain*, with conclusions which are quite startling.

Of Perthshire, in the areas of the MacGregor country, he says that many of the inhabitants resembled the Caledonians of Tacitus' description, of large athletic frame and red hair. But these were in a minority and he thinks that they were also in a minority in Roman times, and that Tacitus noted them because they were outstanding. But over the whole area, Beddoe said, the population was more homogeneous than he had found in any similar area he had investigated. In short he considered that the inhabitants (though each one, like every other human, was individually unique) had not, in general, changed their characteristics for at least eighteen centuries. They had remained a tightly compacted community. He wrote that they showed strong attachment, a love of nature and of poetry, shrewdness and wit and a martial spirit, allied to physical fitness, and ability to endure hunger, thirst, cold, heat and fatigue.

So, surprisingly we find that, despite the ravages of persecution, (though, not all of them being MacGregors, some escaped this) the clearances, the suppression of Celtic culture by the Hanoverians and Presbyterians, the emigrations to the industrial belt, these Central Highlanders of a century ago (before the Railway Age began to bite), though much reduced in numbers, remained true to ancient tradition. This was the genetic reservoir to which I referred in my introduction.

How they originally came to this area, and of what races were the previous inhabitants with whom they had to contend when they arrived, I can only make the wildest surmises, which I shall spare my reader. In the Folk Wandering Ages, of which there were several at long intervals, incredible things happened, sometimes dictated by the polity of Rome and sometimes at the whim of a barbarian tribe. The Jews, after the second destruction of the Temple in 70 AD, were scattered as prisoners to every far corner of the Empire; Germanic tribes like the Heruli trekked through the borders of the Empire and destroyed the wonderful monuments of Athens; the Picts reduced Roman London to a smoking ruin in the 4th century AD. It is not wise to limit the possibilities of the origins of nations.

Finghin's visit to John XIII started something which, had that Pope been gifted with second sight, would have given him bad dreams.

Chapter 6. Abbots with Iron Habits.

'Onward, Christian soldiers!' was no mere figure of speech in the Middle Ages. The Columban and other monks not only risked martyrdom, they sought it, without resorting to weapons. In Scotland and Ireland, during the Viking raids, the ecelesiasts built the very tall round towers which still defy the attacks of weather and time. But with the abbots, who were responsible for a large community, it began to be impressed on them that they would need to play a more militant role.

Two years before Finghin went to Rome, the Annals of the Scots record the fall in battle of Duncan, Abbot of Dunkeld, along with Dubdou, the satrap or thane of Atholl. Later in this chapter we find the same association of Church and local ruler.

In 1045, Crinan, another Abbot of Dunkeld, the son-in-law of that King Malcolm II who had preceded Duncan MacCrinan as king, led a rebellion against MacBeth in the interests of his own family. MacBeth defeated and slew him. (Duncan MacCrinan also was slain by MacBeth as all the world knows.)

The Abbots were men of politics as well as of God. They had to be, for, apart from civil quarrels, the different church disciplines struggled with each other for centuries. The early idea of a purely spiritual Christianity was renewed in the 10th century by the Pictish Church, which renamed itself the Cele De (friends of God), or Culdee, and consequently opposed the further Romanising of their church by the appointment of bishops subject to the papal authority. As I said earlier, King Nechtan had already conceded something to Roman forms.

But no church was free of 'the contagion of the world's slow stain.' It corrupted even the Culdees.

When Saint Margaret, wife of the unspeakable barbarian Malcolm III (Canmore), met the Culdees in the 11th century she admired their spirituality. But Abbots arose who forgot their obligations to God and their community. More and more they laid claim to the lands and goods of the monasteries and abbeys, whose revenues, following the principles laid down by Charlemagne, were due to be devoted to the furtherances of scholarship. These Abbots absented themselves on secular business. Many of them became clan chiefs and in this capacity raised private armies, and also robbed the clansmen of their rightful land, which the chief was expected to conserve for the common good.

Here is an instance of how this vicious system worked. The O'Beollans became secular lairds in Wester Ross because they possessed the monastic lands of Abercrossan. With their formidable forces they supported the Scotic kings, and, in return, their descendants were made hereditary Earls of Ross.

The facts of documented history show that this secularising movement was widespread, and the worldly ambitions of some Abbots knew no bounds.

Not all churchmen followed these bad examples. But it is of direct bearing on the Clans Gregor, MacKinnon and MacNab that in the long reign of William I, the Lion, 1165–1214, the 'Abbot' of Glen Dochart was a layman who was associated in a legal record of William I with the Earl of Atholl, so he was a fairly powerful man. The extract reads '*Comitem Atholie vel ad Abbatem de Clendrochard*.' Very much more significant than this, however, is the fact that through the whole of William's reign there is no record of any monastery in Glen Dochart, Celtic or otherwise, so 'Abbot of Clendrochard' was an empty title, as well as a hypocritical one.

The Bagimond Roll was a financial record of tithes ordered by Pope Gregory X in his magnificent but vain effort to restore a former character of universality and political superiority to the Papacy. All the ecclesiastic foundations in Scotland were entered, with their valuations. The purpose of these tenths or tithes was to supply funds for a new Crusade. Our interest in this statement is in the fact that there is no entry against Glen Dochart for the years of the Roll, 1275–78. There are entries of the Vicarage of Comrie; the Church of Balquhidder, the Abbey or Abthanerie of Aberfoyle, the Abbey of Inch Affray on the Earn, and the Abbey of Iona. (The Vikings had long since stopped their molestation of Iona and the Battle of Largs, twelve years before the Roll, had started a regression of Norse influence.) The first four of these entries in the Bagimond Roll were all in the MacGregor country, so the absence of Glen Dochart proves that the 'Abbots' had been lay chiefs for well over a century.

The Bagimond, or Baiamond's Roll, was not printed in book form until 1864, and even in that state it is rare, but is of value in tracing the origins of the clans, many of whom, originating in abthaneries, by the end of the thirteenth century had become quite secular. It is also of interest, indirectly, because Edward I tried to commandeer the Scottish tithes, but could not get them until after the death of Alexander III.

A Roll of a different character, which was a kind of Traitors' Charter, was the Rageman's or Ragman's Roll, made up twenty years after Baiamond's Roll. This time it was not Pope Gregory X who ordered it, but Edward I, who was engaged in subduing the British Isles to form an English Empire. Wallace was waging war, in an attempt, at first very successful, to get rid of the English army of occupation and the horde of officials of all sorts who were intruding into civil and ecclesiastic offices. The Ragman's Roll was a long list of all sorts of Scottish landholders who, willingly or not, paid homage to Edward for land. The derogatory expression 'rigmarole' was derived from this list, and shows the contempt in which it was ultimately held.

Edward firmly believed in his destiny, even to the extent of expressing a wish to return the Stone of Destiny to Scone; but the citizens of London strongly objected. Edward's generosity was merely a mask for his real purpose, which was to have himself crowned King of the Scots upon the Stone, in much the same way as Kenneth MacAlpin had used the Stone in the 9th century to be recognised as monarch of the Picts. Edward very nearly succeeded, for he managed to persuade Balliol and many powerful families, such as the Bruces, to support him. But the barbarity and arrogance of the English army and officials caused the Wallace revolt, in which he was supported by most of the Highland clans.

At the Battle of Dunbar in 1296, Edward was reinforced by the Earl of Dunbar, Robert Bruce and the Annandale clans, and other auxiliaries not of English birth. Against him were ranged the Earls of Buchan with the Comyns, Lennox with the powerful MacDougals and John MacGregor of Glen Orchy with a most formidable gathering; the Earl of Mar led the Gordons, the Forbeses and the Farquharsons. Many of these had signed the Ragman's Roll, amongst them John of Glen Orchy, but had repented.

Unluckily Edward won the battle, though he did not subdue the Scottish opposition, who escaped through the intricacies of the boggy Lammermoor Hills, close by. John MacGregor must have been unwilling to extract himself from the close conflict, for he was captured and held to ransom, which in itself shows that he was either recognised or made himself known. No money was demanded, as far as is known. But before he was set free he had to give a guarantee that he would pay homage to Edward for his lands in Glen Orchy. This did not mean that Edward was King of Scotland. It only meant that, legally, Edward was acting as superior until a new monarch could be instituted by the Seven Earls of Scotland, who were direct inheritors of the Seven Thegns, Maormors, or sub-kings of Pictavia. On the (presumed) death of the Maid of Norway, the heir to Alexander III, these Earls recognised the heirs of Robert Bruce of Annandale, who had already been recognised by Alexander II and the Earls, as heir presumptive. Alexander III paid homage to Edward I for lands in Tynedale, Cumberland and Westmorland; Edward himself paid homage to Philip IV for the lands of Guienne. It was quite in order for John MacGregor to pay homage for Glen Orchy.

This casual information tells us, by deduction, that the MacGregors, before 1296, had moved westward from Glen Dochart and were in possession of lands in Dalriada; these were in Glen Orchy, and in the glens around Loch Awe. They may well have taken these from tribes of Dalriadic Scots, or perhaps may have become landlords of the aboriginal people whose forebears came from Dalriada in Ulster in the sixth century.

Another condition of John MacGregor's release was that he would bring his forces to support Edward I in his wars in France with Philip IV, the Fair, over his claim to the sovereignty of Guienne. But, although Miss A. G. M. MacGregor, in her *History*, thinks that John probably died in France shortly after 1296, this is not supported by history. Pope Boniface VIII managed to arrange a truce between the French and English kings at that time, and awarded Edward the disputed province, so there was no cause for the MacGregors to leave Scotland. They were required, however, to promise not to take up arms against Edward. No doubt they found ways to continue their support of Wallace in the subsequent battles of Stirling Bridge and Falkirk. But there is good reason to think they shared in the awards of lands and money, £100 (an enormous sum), which Edward gave to Dougal MacDougal of Lorne to support him against Bruce.

Bruce did not delay in seeking retribution from those who opposed him. Shortly after his coronation he gave the Earl of Strathearn (Malise) a promise of safe conduct to a conference with him, where he tried to get him to break his oath of allegiance to Edward. On Malise refusing to break his pledged word, Bruce revoked his safe-conduct promise, imprisoned Malise, sent Atholl into Strathearn to ravage and destroy it. Only on threat of beheadal did Malise break his allegiance to Edward. The MacDougalls and MacGregors were to be dealt with in similar fashion by Bruce and his successors.

Chapter 7. MacGregors Hold Three Kings.

We have now arrived at a point of time, somewhere in the high Middle Ages, when the Glen Orchy, or most powerful and aggressive, branch of Clan Gregor, has a chief with no connection, other than titular or even nominal, with the Glen Dochart monastery, which is now obsolete. He is recognised in British affairs as a Scottish landowner on a par with thanes and earls. He even claims to be in the direct line of ancient kings, and perhaps, on that account, his life is spared in defeat, and he is allowed to give his word of honour that he will, if required, bring his forces to support Edward abroad.

Apparently, though there must have been opposition to the expansion of the Clan Gregor westwards and northwards from its original territories, their right of the sword, or in Gaelic, *Còir a Chlaidheamh*, was an argument too strong to resist. But towards the end of the fourteenth century a new power was emerging from the heart of Dalriada, now Argyll. This was the Clan Campbell, who had already disputed the sovereignty of Kintyre and Knapdale with the MacDougals, and had secured a strong foothold in Cowal, the hereditary territory of the Lamonts. In 1390 John MacGregor, Cham, the skelly-eyed, had died and through circumstances rather confused, but perhaps involving shady legal transactions, one of the Campbell lairds took over the title of Glen Orchy. This was hotly disputed by the descendants of John Cham, his sons Patrick, John and Gregor: the latter two being designated John the Black and Gregor MacAne. The son of Iain Dubh (John the Black) was Callum or Malcolm, probably now having a very hard struggle with the Campbells and Stewarts. About his time a Gaelic table of genealogy of the chiefs was committed to a document which still exists. This was possibly an attempt to prove that as a direct descendant of an ancient king of Dalriada, (Fergus Fada), the Clan Gregor chief had a right to Glen Orchy. If it was adduced as evidence, it was swept aside by the Campbells in their zest to acquire more land, at the expense of the clan who persisted in trying to hold it without feudal charters.

Some time after this list of 1467, another claim to royal origins was written. This was by Duncan MacGregor, brother of James MacGregor, Dean of Lismore. In some ways his line of ancestry agrees with its predecessor, of whose existence he was probably well aware, as no doubt he was, also, of another list of earlier date to either, written about 1440 by a contemporary of Callum, the grandson of Iain Cham.

In the immediate past of ancestry, back for six generations, (or at any rate six Tanists, or male successors) to Duncan beag (the younger) who was chief in the early 13th century, all writers agree with one another. W. R. Kermack, in his hand-book *The Clan MacGregor*, submits a re-arrangement which seems very feasible, but he, also, agrees with the above tables.

When we begin to go farther back it gradually dawns on us that the lines of the 1467 and the 1512 lists are not at all running parallel. In fact they are branching off to stations that are quite remote from one another in time, space and race. Leaving out the six chiefs that all are agreed upon, I write the lists back in time as they occur in two of the manuscripts.

Gaelic M.S. of 1467	Gaelic M.S. of 1512
Gilchrist	Duncan
Fergus	Gioll Fialaidh (hospitable)
Murdoch	Hugh of Urchy (Orchy)
Andrew	Kenneth Alpin (died 837)
Cormac	
Airbertach	
Fergus Og	
Fergus Fada (died 697)	

The first thing to look at is the credibility of the lists. They seem to cover two long periods, the 1467 list from about 1150, at the latest, back to 697, when Fergus Fada is known to have died. This makes about 450 years which would give each chief an average potential of 56 years. The 1512 list from about the same time, 1150, covers 300 years, giving an average of 60 years for each. When one compares this with the later chiefs whose dates are fairly well known, from their association with events like the battle of Dunbar, we find the John of that event (1296) whose branch ended with his daughter Margaret or Mariota, is two generations anterior to John of Glenorchy of a collateral branch who died in 1390; again an average of 50 years or so. In respect of length of their lives, the lists of older generations appear feasible, though their longevity strains our belief somewhat.

A difficulty seems to arise over the Chief Hugh, or Eochy, of Urchy, who is claimed to be the son of Kenneth MacAlpin. The name Hugh is very likely to prove something about his Scotic ancestry, for it was a Dalriadic name and the name of the notorious Hugh the Poisonous, father of Alpin. In the Annals of the Scots for 940, as I mentioned in Part 1, Chapter 2, the death of Hugh MacAlpin is recorded. I put the question there, 'why was he not allowed to succeed Donald?' who was his brother, by some accounts.

Possibly the answer to this question is, because he was given a sub-kingdom in Lorn, the north of Dalriada, which includes Glen Orchy, and he was a Tanist; not a son of Kenneth, but his brother. There was certainly not a Clan Gregor at that time, as I have shown, but this does not affect Hugh's rule over Glen Orchy, which was probably populated by Dalriadic Scots whom the MacGregors displaced over a century later. But there may well be a generation or two missing in the list.

We have now got a regal bonus for the MacGregor Chiefs. They have claimed, by these two divergent lines of descent, a double stake in royal origins, both, however of Scotic or half-Scotic kings; which still does not prevent the clan over whom they later claimed headship from proclaiming itself possibly also of royal descent, but from the Pictish ruler, Gregor MacDungal, of the Picto-Scottish kingdom. Well may the Clan Gregor motto be ''S Rìoghail mo Dhrèam' (Regal is my family).

To some people, who have perhaps seen the ridiculous genealogies which fanatical Milesians have amassed from fabulous regions of time, going back meticulously to Noah's Ark or, as has been quipped, to a rival vessel of Celtic construction, the above family tree may appear only a rigmarole. But it ties in with many authenticated chronicles and the obscurity of parts of it may quite well be attributed to our ignorance. As the average reign of each chief is so great in extent, there could not have been many brothers claiming to be Tanists. Most of the succession must have been father to son.

As to the credibility of the lists, it is not irrelevant to refer to a typical non-Celtic view, that of Matthew Arnold. His judgements were often proved radically wrong, but that did not prevent him from publishing the dictum that the 'Celts in general were always ready to react against the despotism of fact.' He probably meant only the British Celts, the Welsh, Irish and Scottish Gaels, who undeniably have infused English literature with rich images. But they were only tattered remnants of the great Celtic race which, in the 5th century BC, when Rome was a cluster of brigands' hovels, had built up a superb culture in all fields of metal techniques, and had expanded centrifugally from the heartland of Europe into Asia Minor, Africa and Western Europe. They did not do this on imagination alone, nor is their history a fiction. If they chose to cultivate the inexhaustible riches of the human mind, and memorised what other races committed to brick, stone and parchment, they showed the same wisdom as the Jews in adversity, who taught their children by rote to memorise their history and laws. The Celts thought it unworthy to commit anything to writing.

One of the greatest Scottish poets was illiterate and, as such, despised by his inferiors in intellectual ability. He was Duncan Ban MacIntyre, a native of Glen Orchy, who was employed as a gamekeeper when he was composing his great epics and lyrics in the recesses of Ben Doran. In his old age he was employed at sixpence a day to be a City Guardsman in the Edinburgh of the much lauded Golden Age, whose illustrious ornaments of the arts were unaware that such a poet was performing his daily drudgery amongst them. Well has the age of printing been described as the Tyranny of Gutenberg. The lists of the MacGregor chiefs had been memorised by successive generations of seanachaidh, reciters of old records and stories. They were liable to human error but they are much more trustworthy than many of the monastic chroniclers.

The most important point for comment on the list of 1467 is its origin in Farquhar, or Ferchair Fada. Our own royal family also claim descent from him, by way of Kenneth MacAlpin, Robert Bruce, and James VI. But when one considers the reprehensible usurpations of Alpin and of Kenneth; the barbarities, accompanied by murder of relatives, by Malcolm Canmore; the claims of Bruce, whose Scotic blood was barely traceable; the line of Bruce broken into by the Stuarts; the generally believed bastardy of Robert III, and also the very dubious parentage of James VI, their descent from Farquhar is very uncertain.

In the confused state of Scotland in the last third of the 15th century, when James III was still a minor and all sorts of claimants, backed often by English interests, were squabbling for the Scottish throne, the MacGregor chief's document was probably treated with contempt. The land robbing continued with diligence, in the absence of an effective system of law, and the accompanying slaughter intensified, for the Clan Gregor did not take it lying down.

To afford a little light relief to this question of royal succession, I would like to introduce a military adventurer of Sir Walter Scott's time. He had been the right-hand man of Simón Bolívar in the savage wars of Venezuelan liberation and was named Sir Gregor MacGregor, to whom I later refer. He published a book to promote his proposed new Darien Scheme in 1821–3. His lieutenant, Mr. Strangeways, was the sponsor of the book in which is printed a magnificent etching of Sir Gregor in full military rig-out, described as 'His Majesty Gregor, Cacique (chief) of the Poyais Indians in Mosquitia'. He proclaims that he can trace his descent faithfully back to Kenneth MacAlpine, King of the Scots, and therefore has a full claim to the Throne of Great Britain, ('usurped' at that time by the 'First Gentleman of Europe', George IV). I wonder that a reputable publisher should bring this out, and also wonder what Sir Walter, the adulator of George IV, thought privately about this presumptuous devil that his spells had helped to raise out of his native heath.

All the same, the Cacique of Poyitia had more than a grain of truth in his boasting, for he was of the house of Glen Gyle. His grandfather was Gregor Glun Dhubh (Gregor of the black spot on the knee), a nephew and ward of Rob Roy. This Glen Gyle branch claimed descent from Malcolm of Glen Orchy. Glun Dhubh's epitaph, in Glen Gyle burial-ground begins,

'Not with vain flattery to insult the dead
We place this stone above thy honour'd head'

Little doubt exists that the composer of these noble pentameters knew very well the royal claims of this and other families of Clan Gregor.

Chapter 8. Great Oaks from Small Acorns.

Earlier in this book I referred to 'King' Achaius whom J. H. Burton deflated rather harshly, though with some justification. During the period when Scotland was still struggling against the attempts of England to extinguish its independence, there arose a school of Scots propagandists who went about Europe blowing trumpets to inform the nations of the supreme qualities of the Scots. They temporarily suppressed the fact that the Scots were unwanted immigrants from Ireland in the early centuries, and when any of these Irish Scots, such as Erigena, achieved the peak of intellectual power, and was acclaimed in the universities of Europe, these propagandists of the sixteenth century or thereabouts pounced upon this paragon for the national gallery, though it was certain that Erigena had only seen the hills of 'Scotland' or Alba on a clear day across the North Channel. In the 9th century, when he flourished, there was no Scotland.

In the same way the claims of the Scottish kings to royal origins, and in our case, of the clan Gregor chiefs to this source, were blown up out of all proportion. We are reminded of the fable of Aesop where the frog inflates himself in his desire to be a bull, until he bursts. This is the true bragging of the Gael, which has infected all Scots in their anxiety to keep their end up, in the face of the imperturbable assurance and unassuming arrogance of English superiority. 'Here's tae us; wha's like us? Damn few, and they're a' deid.' That toast puts it in a nutshell. Most Scots treat it as a joke, however, but in late mediaeval times the Scots encomiasts, Fordun,

Buchanan and numerous others took a serious view. It was only in the beginning of a more truth-loving century, the 18th, that a pragmatical Aberdonian priest, Father Thomas Innes, who had to go abroad to publish his debunking of national myths, *Critical Essay on the Early Inhabitants of Scotland* in 1729, threw a bucket of cold water on these feverish imaginings.

To confer the title 'King' upon Fergus is to do him rather too much honour. His name in Gaelic means 'honest man' and we all associated this at school with Pope's 'An honest man's the noblest work of God', and Burns' 'Is there for honest poverty that hings his heid, and a' that?' Fergus had no prophetic view of how over-spreading an oak was to develop in the fullness of centuries from his humble acorn. He had a hard job staying alive for he was disputing the 'Kingship' of Dalriada with Hugh MacHugh. Fergus ruled over Lorne, the northern part which extends from Glen Orchy to the Firth of Lorne: Hugh ruled Knapdale and the long moorish peninsula of Kintyre. They bickered with one another all their reigns, and each knew his fate, should he be conquered.

The Scots did not co-operate with one another. After Fergus's death in 697, his two sons fought each other for supremacy, and the loser had his throat cut. *'Jugulatus'* and *'jugulati'* are words that keep on appearing in the annals of Dalriada. They need no translation, nor thinking about. Anarchy prevailed in Dalriada as well as elsewhere until (many years after Fergus was gathered to his long home in Iona) Angus the Pictish king made a desert of Dalriada and called it peace, burning all the towns. At the so-called 'Beregonium', at Benderloch, the vitrified stones of the ancient Scotic hill-fort may still be seen, to commemorate this, or perhaps a similar atrocity by the Vikings, later in time.

I have shown earlier how the Scots employed all sorts of stratagems to ensure their sovereignty when they took over the Pictish Kingdom. In that larger territory they expanded, and, by conquest, they spread their form of Celtic to all parts of Scotland except Lothian where, by an agreement between Kenneth II and King Edgar in 970, the Anglians of Lothian, whose remoteness from the main Northumbrian kingdom made them an embarrassment, were joined to the Scottish crown with the provisos that they were to retain their own customs, laws and language. Many Gaelic place-names were, nevertheless, transposed upon the Anglian and Old Welsh names, to the confusion of the later mapmakers, who knew no Celtic of either P or Q kind.

Probably the biggest bit of Scotic trumpet-blowing was inspired by the overwhelming efforts of Edward I and II to conquer, or, in some subtler way, to gain dominion. This was the famous Declaration of Arbroath of 1320 when the Scots clergy and noblemen, irrespective of Robert Bruce, declared their firm resolution to retain the integrity of Scotland. It will be noticed that 'Scotland' was the description of the land which for so many ages had been called Alban, or Alba, and the title of the King, (which even Farquhar the Long and his Dalriadic rulers assumed rather, prematurely) was no longer *'Ri Albain'*. This title ended with MacBeth, the last of the kings of mixed Scotic and Pictish blood. A new race of kings, of Saxon and Norman origins, now called themselves 'Kings of the Scots', which perhaps they were in some small degree, at the expense of pushing the Angles, Britons, Picts, Danes and Norse out of the picture. But they, personally, and least of all the Normans amongst them, could not claim to be Scots in the racial sense, a very vague catalogue, any more than that they were descended from that mysterious mummy Scota, daughter of the Pharaoh who was drowned in the Red Sea in 1491 BC, a miracle which perhaps suggested St. Cuthbert's earthquake of 885 AD.

Yet, believing themselves to be 'a chosen nation with a special part in the divine plan and a mission to convert the world', the Scotic party engaged Bernard de Linton, a learned churchman, to compose a grandiloquent address to the Pope, or rather the Anti-pope, Johannes XXII, whose predecessor Clement V had transferred the papal centre to Avignon, in the 'Babylonian Exile'.

Dante was not entirely unprejudiced, as a close reading of *Inferno*, *Purgatorio* and *Paradiso* reveals. For example, he thought Edward I of England a splendidly just king. Perhaps Edward was, initially, but his later oppressions and illegal acts cannot be justified in any way. Dante may have favoured Edward because he was at war with Philip the Fair of France, whom Dante disliked. It is interesting, too, that during the revolt of Balliol against Edward I, and the Wallace rebellion, Dante condemned alike the folly of both Scots and English. Still, his description of the Anti-pope to whom the Declaration of Arbroath was directed is worth looking at, for it was written in the last years of Dante's life when he was sad and wise.

In *Paradiso*, Canto XXVII, he described both Anti-popes.

> 'In shepherd's clothing greedy wolves below
> Range wide o'er all the pastures. Arm of God!
> Why longer sleepest thou? Cahorsines and Gascons
> Prepare to quaff our blood.'

Both these rascals were Frenchmen, Clement a Gascon, John from Cahors. They were tools of the French king. It was a waste of good parchment to write to John XXII. His character was notorious, and he was already a hater of Edward II. The only thing he understood was what was to his own advantage. The package deal offered by Bruce's party to support his 'crusade' against the Turks, far outweighed the inflated oratory and bombastic tone of the Declaration.

It has for centuries escaped the observation of our Latinists (Buchanan, if he noticed it, probably turned a blind eye) that the style of the Declaration is mostly a case of borrowed plumes. Anyone conversant with the classical Latin authors can see that the best parts are lifted straight out of Sallust; artificial archaisms, Graecisms, boring moral sermons, fake pre-battle orations, purple platitudes; all are searched for contributions.

This was a gigantic blurb to no purpose. If ever the English king got to read it, and he probably got a copy (for his relationship with Philip the Fair's sons grew hot and cold by turns), he was not persuaded by the truculent tone to desist from attempting to subdue the Scots. It was chiefly the 'scorched-earth' policy of the Scots, and their devastating raids into North England, that turned out to be the expensive arguments listened to by England. I recommend a reading of Sir James Fergusson's learned book on the Declaration.

But any fair-minded person, of whatever nationality, cannot but admire Bruce, despite his murder and sacrilege and devastation of Buchan and Strathearn, and turning his coat politically. He did not have an easy career. Early in his campaign he was hunted like a fox, he had domestic foes even after Bannockburn, including the Humes (Earls of March), FitzGilbert, Carlyle and Colville, as well as the MacGregors, MacDougals etc. But, only a year from early death by disease, he had the satisfaction of signing the double treaty of Edinburgh–Northampton which brought recognition of Scotland's independence (temporarily only). A strange omission in that treaty, which has never been fully explained. is any reference to the return of the Stone of Scone. Perhaps, after all, the Scots preferred to retain their own stone of destiny brought from Dunstaffnage and allowed the Pictish stone to be carried off for keeps by the simple Saxons.

As far as the MacGregor chiefs were concerned, they were bypassed in history and their claim to the Scotic throne was shouldered aside. The Gaelic list claiming royal ancestry was rudely ignored; the wonder is that it survived and can be examined to this day, as a sad reflection on the MacGregors' forlorn hopes. When I was a schoolboy we were taught to despise Kaiser Bill, and the slogans 'Might is Right' and 'God is on the side of the big battalions' (Voltaire). Now, in my maturer period, I sadly agree with the French cynic as far as the MacGregor chiefs are concerned. They were early given to understand that Scotland had no place or use for them. At Flodden, as I shall tell in detail later, the most warlike man of the Clan Gregor, who could have brought a very effective body of his experienced clan to aid the vacillating James IV, was imprisoned underground in Campbell of Glen Orchy's prison, awaiting beheadal. He had so little patriotism that he greatly rejoiced to hear of Glen Orchy's death by the side of his king: what would any of us have done in his case?

Chapter 9. The Line of Chiefs Inspected.

The lineage of the MacGregor chiefs of Glen Orchy being one of the few certain claims of this family back into the earliest centuries, it is profitable to make as many inferences as we can from the names without assuming any unwarrantable position.

The list, imperfect as it is, proves that the Glenorchy chiefs were of Scotic origin, even if we exclude their progenitor, for the Scots held to the Scotic law of Tanistry or male succession. In what strange way did they come to claim the leadership of Clan Gregor which I have shown to be of Pictish origin? The MacGregors, along with the MacNabs, MacKinnons, MacQuharries, Grants, MacPhees, MacAlpins, MacAulays and Fergussons of Strachur, all claim to unite in one confederacy, the Siol Alpin. Records corroborate this, though some Norse blood seems to be indicated in MacAulay, son of Olaf or Olaus. Alpin, the name of the confederacy, is not derived from any of the Pictish kings. It is an old Celtic name for Highlands or Alps.

The name list of chiefs gives a clue, though a faint one. The first four of the early names in the 1467 list are all Gaelic which indicates that these men lived among Dalriadic Scots until about the 9th century. Andrew, a biblical name of Greek origin, seems out of place, for it is succeeded by five generations of Gaelic names. It does show however, that they had moved into more generally Picto-Scottish surroundings, for after 761, when St. Andrew was adopted as a patron saint, there may have been a popular move to use his name. The Clan Gregor did not come into being until about the middle of the 11th century at the earliest so, as I indicated above, none of the early so-called MacGregor chiefs has any right to such a title. Assuming fifty years to a name, approximately, and counting back from Malcolm, we see that the very earliest real chief of Clan Gregor on the list could be Fergus, about 1070. But the name Gilchrist, servant of Christ, about 1120 seems more likely to have been an Abbot of Glen Dochart. As there was definitely no monastery or Abthanerie there in 1165, when William I began to reign, Gilchrist may have introduced himself to the clan after 1120 and left it to his successors to become secular 'Abbots', merging into Chiefs. This means that only half of the long line of Malcolm were MacGregor chiefs, or at least, chiefs of the Glen Orchy, or main, tribe. John MacGregor W.S., to whom I referred in my first chapter, contended that no MacGregor family had the prerogative of supplying the chief. If the Clan Gregor kept to the Pictish system of election from the mother's side, they would not feel themselves bound to allow a Tanic custom, but would pick a chief from amongst a wide variety of families. But there is no certainty of this.

The older John on the list, coming into prominence about 1270, is doubtless the John of Glen Orchy, captured by Edward I after Dunbar. His son Gregor early in the next century is the first Gregor in the line. Kermack thinks that this Gregor gave his name to the clan, a hypothesis which, in view of the authentic Gregors of early times, and of the fame of the MacGregors in the previous century (quite apart from Gaelic tradition), I would completely rule out. It is much more likely that Gregor took the name of the clan to make himself more acceptable to them.

Regarding the name Malcolm on the list, a MacGregor chief, or at least a 'Fear-an-tighe' named Malcolm or Calum, was reported by tradition to have borne the nickname 'Lame'. He was reputed to have been a friend of Robert Bruce and to have supported him at Bannockburn. He could not therefore have been the Malcolm MacDuncan of the 12th century, so he must have been of another branch. Certainly he was free to follow Bruce if he so cared, but it is fairly well authenticated that the Argyllshire clans, MacDougals, and Glen Orchy Macgregors, were against Bruce, though they may not have actually opposed him at Bannockburn. The MacNabs, a kindred clan, are recorded as Bruce's foes.

Although it seems inconsistent that a Scotic line of chiefs should put themselves at the head of a Pictish clan, there is nothing unusual in such an arrangement. In fact, following the Celtic manner of landholding, it was common practice that the chief recruited his 'tail', or adherents in battle or raids, from men of a different, or often several different clans from his own. Let me give two examples, drawn from widely separated districts and times.

In 1510, the records of Kintyre, Argyllshire, show that the landlord was a MacDonald chief who granted tacks or rents of land to many families who had in some cases been settled there for centuries. Yet not a single tacksman was a MacDonald, though, by the terms of their tenure, all were expected to follow the MacDonald standard in war.

After Culloden, an account was taken, by a British recorder, of the particulars of the Jacobite dead and wounded, clan by clan, for they fought and fell that way. Of the Stewarts of Appin, the chief's family and chieftain's relatives numbered 22 killed and 25 wounded: of the followers, mostly tacksmen, 69 were killed and 40 wounded; but not one was a Stewart, and they had 18 different surnames.

The above examples seem to suggest that the so-called Clan Gregor may have been heterogeneous. They undoubtedly used different names, apart from their Christian names, and some of the individual names ran to quite a length to distinguish his father, grandfather and any peculiarities among them. The MacIvers, or MacLivers, were of Glen Lyon; the Fletchers or clan of arrow-smiths, inhabited Glen Orchy, as also did the MacGruders, or brewers. The MacNishes or MacNeishes had their abode in Glen Dochart. But they were all MacGregors not far under the skin. After the name was banned they took up at least forty other surnames, so that they could obey the letter of the act, but once again they all knew one another for what they really were.

Probably the Dalriadic chiefs intermarried on occasion with Clan Gregor women and everyone kept a record in memory of the family, if any, and of their career. Old ladies were the usual repositories of such details, and some of these 'caillies' could go back unerringly for a century or more, to recall famous men and their fathers that begat them.

One more point only, which seems puzzling. Since a very ambitious family made themselves chief of Clan Gregor, or, at least, assumed this distinction and were generally accepted, why did they not insist that the clan should take its name from King Fergus or Farquhar. (There is however a branch of the Siol Alpin, related to MacGregors, named the Fergussons of Strachur.) The fact that the clan retained the name Gregor seems to point to a strong lobbying at the time of the takeover, whenever it was; we shall never know any more about this matter beyond the likelihood that there were a good many very stiff-necked clansmen, whom no power on earth was going to deprive of 'The Name'. They went on to prove it beyond any argument. The MacAlpins, a closely related clan, obviously credited their descent from Alpin through Hugh of Orchy (Gaelic, Urcha) or his descendants.

Part 2. Landless.

Chapter 1. 'This Beast is Mischievous!'

J. H. Burton, in *The Scot Abroad*, remarking on the clan tournament at Perth between thirty men of each clan, the Clan Kay and Clan Chattan (or, as we might call them, the Mackays and the MacIntoshes) says, 'The Highlanders were in fact the human raw material which a King of Scots could at any time employ for the use or amusement of his guests ... The treatment of the Celts is a blot on that period of our history. Never in later times has the Red Indian or the Australian native been the more hunted wild beast to the emigrant settler than the Highlander was to his neighbour the Lowlander. They were never permitted to be at rest from external assault ... True, he was not easily got at, and, when reached, he was found to have tusks ... Yet, such was their nature that, instead of being pressed by a common cause into compact union, they were divided into communities that hated each other almost more bitterly than they did the common enemy.'

This famous clan tournament, which Scott brought into one of his novels, was witnessed by many European visitors, including Frenchmen, who must have taken back from Scotland a very untrue image of the Celts, deliberately brought into a confrontation like jungle cocks.

It should be noted in this context (the tournament took place at the middle of the reign of that imbecilic dotard Robert III, who in extreme self-pity called himself 'the worst of Kings and the most wretched of men') that it was in the very first year of this reign (1390) that John of Glen

Orchy died, and that his estates passed somehow into the hands of the Campbell lairds. These early Stewart Kings were completely powerless to prevent the rapacity of the Normanised barons, who encroached on the territory of the Highlanders. This policy continued relentlessly for over three centuries, until the final overthrow of the Celts in 1746, when the money from the forfeited estates was partly handed over to those who had helped to destroy the clan system. The Duke of Argyll had supplied 3,000 levies to support Cumberland. Their main part in the battle of Culloden was to throw down a dry-stane dyke, to allow the cavalry through to cut down the fleeing Jacobites. But, with the blood-money from the forfeitures, the Duke was able to complete Inveraray Castle in 1747 in a sufficiently magnificent style, although his execrable taste in choosing, and abusing, a classical line from Vergil to adorn the foundation stone, was commented on very scathingly by Dr. King of St. Mary's Hall, Oxford, a Tory of the time. Vergil's line was '*Deus nobis haec otia fecit*', God hath provided us with these comforts. But Argyll had the double distinction, according to Dr. King, of offending his Creator and spoiling a hexameter at the same stroke by substituting Dux Cumbriae, the Duke of Cumberland, for God. This acknowledgement of thanks is probably not very conspicuous to visitors.

How this enmity between Highlander and Lowlander arose is not to be easily explained, but one of the principal reasons was assuredly the resistance of the Celts to the Norman feudal idea. In Ireland, where a great plain is surrounded by mountains, with regular gaps between, so that no resistance to invasion is practicable, the native Celts were easily subdued by the Norman invasions of the twelfth century, and the eventual overthrow of the Celtic system was merely delayed by occasional rebellion. But, in the Scottish Highlands, the mountains presented an impenetrable barrier to the movements of heavily armoured horse and foot on which the Normanised Lowlanders relied. As for the building of keeps and castles, complete with dungeons, torture-chambers and all the accessories of iron-bound tyranny, this could only be attempted where the work could proceed within easy access to building material and, more important, freedom from attack while building was going on.

The Highlanders did not need to build strongholds; nature had provided them in superfluity. One has only to look north from the Midland Valley, from such splendid view-points as Arthur's Seat, Edinburgh, or Stirling Castle, or from the top storey of one of Glasgow's multi-storey flats when the wind blows from the Highlands and the air is crystal-clear. Yonder lie the blue hills of the Highlands, like the waves of a tumultuous ocean, edged with white on the peaks of Ben Lomond, Ben More, Schiehallion, stretching away in countless hundreds into apparent infinity.

They inspire us now with boundless joy and pride in our heritage but the sight of them to the mediaeval or early modern Lowlander was quite the contrary. It was an unknown territory, the natives spoke a language, if it deserved such a distinguished description, which sounded like the shrieking of devils in pandemonium, exacerbated by the moans and drones and screeches of bagpipes. They were hostile, treacherous, and uncivilised, given to murder and robbery without provocation. That was a dreadful picture to have constantly in mind when one glanced at the lovely Caledonian bens and glens. In *Rob Roy* we are permitted, through the eyes of Bailie Nicol Jarvie, to see a fairly true impression of the Highlands as viewed from the Sautmarket, i.e., the burghs of Scotland.

But the above picture of barbarism is scarcely justified. The Highlanders, in the main, before they began to be driven to bay, were peacefully employed in keeping their flocks and herds, hunting and fishing, cultivating small areas of oats or barley, cutting and drying hay, preparing fuel by cutting peats and brushwood against the winter, weaving, iron-working for domestic or hunting utensils. In the recreational activities, piping, singing, composing verses, playing games of skill or prowess, performing athletic feats were all enjoyed as occasion arose. For the intellectually inclined it must not be thought they were deprived of any opportunity. In early mediaeval times, and until the anti-Celtic persecutions began in the fifteenth century, the abthaneries provided opportunity to study. At Dull or Dall, in the fertile Strath of Appin close to where the River Lyon joins the Tay, almost under the shadow of Schiehallion, the most regularly shaped mountain in Britain, there was maintained a university under the rule of the abthanerie of Dull. So celebrated was this seat of learning, from the earlier part of the high Middle Ages until the fifteenth century, that it was protected from molestation by being made a sanctuary equal in prestige to Holyrood, and the nearby village of Dull was made an open town, similar to the unwalled burgh of Herbergere, or the Canongate, under protection from the church.

A different story now. Even the memory of this seat of learning in the heart of MacGregor country has vanished. Between 1831 and 1861 the population of the parish dropped from 4,500 to under 3,000, due to the second wave of clearances. The same tale can be repeated ad nauseam. The 'mischievous beasts' have fled from their old stamping grounds.

Fifty years ago I walked and camped through this whole countryside, dressed in the kilt, and raising fire and boiling water by the Orchy, the Tummel and the Keltney Burn. It looked like a natural wilderness, but of course I knew it was not. Every now and again there were larachs, or heaps of stone and lime, where the clansfolk had persisted for two millennia and more. Glen Orchy and the great hill of Ben Doran, where Duncan Ban ranged through all its ferny and leafy recesses after the deer, was a vast and awe-inspiring wilderness on the fresh breezy August morning in 1928. I had it all to myself, except for one or two hoodie crows trying to pick a living. Here was the land of John MacGregor, last laird of his line, the territory of the Fletchers, the scene of 'sundry slauchteris done by the clangregoure' and against them, also. Well, it was very peaceful, but it was a desert. Agricola, Edward Bruce, or Cumberland couldn't have improved on it.

Having arrived in Glen Orchy, the scene of the first of the Clan Gregor's land losses, I think I shall commence the narration of the MacGregor's age-long resistance to extermination from there, in my next chapter.

Chapter 2. A Caledonian Crusade.

The Highland clans take a great pride in their antiquity. An old Gaelic proverb says, 'MacDonald as the heather, MacGregor as the rock'. Like the chicken and egg it is arguable which came first. Another saying is, 'As old as the hills, the Devil, and the MacArthurs'. The MacArthurs, a Campbell sept, are very ancient, no doubt, but their two competitors were here before them, and the clan was not descended from King Arthur, slain, according to the annals, at Camlan, place not known, in 537 AD. There were clans among the Picts and Scots before then, but they were of a different nature from the Highland clans of Scotland, though no doubt the idea was the same and the word *clann*, meaning children, described them. The reason for the great anxiety to be older than the neighbouring clan was probably to prove a prior right to the territory. First come, first served. The squabble will never end as we know only too well when we look at the situation in the Near East. Let us imagine that the Welsh decided that they would re-claim '*Y Gogledd*', the Lost North, or the whole of the South of Scotland, including Glasgow and Edinburgh, all of which was owned by Old Welsh or British tribes as well as the whole of England. Could it happen here?

Another proverbial saying, to come back exactly to what concerns us in this book, is, in Gaelic, ''*Se clann gobha-na-saighead a thog a cheud smùid a thug goil air uisge na Urcha*', The clan of the arrow-smiths were the first to raise smoke and boil water from the Orchy. This was often asserted by the Fletchers, a sept of Clan Gregor, though it is hard to believe it, for there must have been very ancient pre-Celtic tribes there, perhaps of Bronze Age immigrants or earlier. Still, the old saying may show that the Fletchers were there before the

Campbells, though history does not need a traditional saying to prove it right.

Alasdair Alpin MacGregor in *Wild Drumalbain* tells how the Fletchers lost their lands by trickery. Black Duncan Campbell, with two accomplices, rode up to Achallader and all three put their horses to feed in Fletcher's uncut corn which was ready for the sickle. Fletcher rushed out and slew one of the trespassers. Being forced to flee from the law, he was kindly offered a chance to preserve his lease by lending it to Campbell until he could safely return. Needless to say, he could never persuade Campbell to give back his lease.

This was a well-rehearsed trick of the Campbell family to which Black Duncan belonged. One of the early Campbell countesses, or duchesses, at Inveraray, used to ask a loan of charters from the neighbouring landholders on the pretext of studying them. They were never returned and the greed of this particular family became proverbial over the Inveraray district for some of the cheated families were also Campbells.

There is said to be a knoll at Achallader, Alasdair Alpin says, which is still called the *'cnoc'* of the stranger and marks the grave of Campbell's unlucky accomplice.

This is only one incident, a minor one, in hundreds of similar filchings of crofts and parcels of land, from a rental of one or two marks to whole glens and straths, over the centuries, very few of these robberies unaccompanied by blood-spilling.

In 1453, the Exchequer Rolls have incidental notes about spoilation and slaughter by Clan Gregor, and significantly, in 1488, an act of Council gave powers to Campbell of Glen Orchy, Stewart of Fothergill and Campbell of Glen Falloch to pursue and destroy the raiding bands of MacGregors. Although the earliest rental rolls of the area designate MacGregors as vassals of Campbell of Glen Orchy, and of Argyll (the Earl) from 1390 to 1590, this only seems to indicate that prior to the death of the chief, John MacGregor, in 1390, the MacGregors, Fletchers and other septs possessed the entire region. Margaret, heiress of John MacGregor, captured at Dunbar, had married John Campbell of Loch Awe but Glen Orchy had reverted for a time to the MacGregors because of the death of Campbell's heir.

The encroachment of the Dalriadic Campbell lairds on the 'Three Glens', Orchy, Lochy and Strae, began in earnest then, at the end of the 14th century, which was once more, like the 8th and 9th centuries, a period of anarchy in Scotland under the ineffective kings Robert II and Robert III. The wars of Edward I and Edward II had thrown Scotland back a long way. Some historians say a century, but, for a comparative reign of brutality and misery, one would fail to find a similar period later than the days of Viking devastation. The Three Hundred Years War with the 'Auld Enemy', England, was being waged with mixed fortunes and a reduction to a desert of the Merse of Berwickshire and all Northumberland and Durham.

Of course there was the brief glory portrayed in ballads like 'Otterburn' and 'Harlaw', but these were only local skirmishes, after all, between raiders out for personal gain. To counterbalance this there was famine, even cannibalism, and universal misery. The Golden Age of Alexander III was a lost dream. There is known to have been an amelioration of the climate during the 12th and 13th centuries. That gave way to another 'Little Ice Age', similar to the 'Seven Winters' which ended the 17th century. The MacGregors were not the only people persecuted, if that was but scanty consolation to them.

By 1440 they had lost most of their Argyllshire lands, including Kilchurn Castle, one of their ancient strongholds, on the accessible east side of Loch Awe. Colin Campbell, ancestor of Black Duncan of the Cowl (or hood) now became first Laird of Glenorchy. He did not exterminate all the inhabitants, Fletchers, MacGruders, MacGregors, or MacNabs (as the Stewarts did with the MacIvers or MacLivers, a MacGregor sept of Glen Lyon), but they had to acknowledge his overlordship. As late as 1648 a John MacConachie VcGruder of Ardtaitle in Glen Orchy had two cows stolen by a John Ross, of Wachtermalzie, who was hanged for it. A family of MacNab blacksmiths are known to have resided in Glen Orchy until the 18th century. Sir Colin's wife employed members of that family to do ironwork in the renovated Kilchurn Castle while her husband, in Alasdair Alpin's phrase 'was absent at the Crusades ... on his seven years sojourn in the Holy Land.'

If I may be allowed a small digression, I should like to put right an unsupportable fable about 'Sir Colin the Crusader'. Briefly, the last legitimate Crusade petered out around 1270, a century and a half before Colin's day. Money was raised (as I detailed in my paragraph on the Bagimond's Roll) by Gregory X, for a Final Crusade in 1275–78, but the cash was stolen by Edward I and Charles of Anjou, so the Crusade never got off the ground. The spirit of Europe at that time was totally averse to Crusades, but disreputable 'Crusades' kept on being preached against heretics and infidels of all sorts, Albigensian Christians in Savoy, Saracens in Spain, Turks in the Balkans. All the riff-raff of mercenaries were enlisted, on Papal promise of loot and full remission of sins, to 'take the Cross' on their back and set out to slaughter or to be slaughtered, perhaps crying 'Christ and no Quarter'. Colin may have taken part in one of these but, as he was a Knight of Rhodes, he probably sojourned there. But he certainly never set foot on the Holy Land. To do so would have landed him in a Turkish jail, for the Ottoman Turks occupied all the mainland, and Rhodes, 600 miles from Jerusalem, was a nest of pirates calling themselves the Knights Hospitallers, whose crusading consisted of attacking merchant shipping, until the Turks made a treaty and evacuated them, long after Sir Colin's day. So, with apologies to the romantic shade of Alasdair, who was a fellow-poet with me in the Twenties, bang goes another myth. But in the official 'Clan Campbell' booklet the fable persists.

Perhaps being immured on Rhodes irritated Sir Colin. When he returned to his renovated castle he began a crusade of a more profitable kind, and enlisted his son and every successor to carry it on. It has been remarked by a visitor to the Scottish National Portrait Gallery that the dynasty of the Glen Orchy Campbells looks like a series of reincarnations of Sir Colin. Their policy never varied. It was 'We'll birse yont' which was said to be the remark of one of them when he built his latest stronghold on the farthest edge of his territory, meaning that he would 'Bash on regardless' into fresh lands to conquer. So just as the crystal waters of the rivers of Savoy were being stained with the blood of 'mothers with infants whose bones lie scattered on the Alpine mountains cold', in Milton's verse, so the clear waters of the Strae, the Orchy and the Lochy were to be reddened with the blood of the heretical MacGregors. But to his irritation he did not find them as meek as lambs led to the slaughter. He had a horde of Tartars, or Turks, by the hands.

Chapter 3. Mary Stuart Enters into her Kingdom.

Dr. Johnson seemed to think that Rob Roy's activities on the shady side of the law brought on the 'annulment' of the name by a legal abolition. But Rob's career was merely an episode in, and not a cause of, the long train of abolitions which began in the reign of Mary, Queen of Scots, in 1563.

To show the extent of the severe acts aimed at destroying the Clan Gregor, and the larger political motives which included this persecution, we must for the moment put aside the encroachments of the house of Breadalbane Campbells on the clan land, which had gone on without intermission for a century and a half before Queen Mary's short reign. Another factor enters the field in the shape of high politics.

Mary Stuart, aged nineteen, arrived back in Scotland in August 1561 and was soon up to her lovely neck in troubles of all sorts. She lacked neither inherited intelligence or acquired cunning, the first from the Stuarts, the second from her mother-in-law, a Medici, for which family, it will be remembered, Machiavelli wrote a secret treatise on statecraft, which caused a bad reaction when it was later published. Little doubt Mary had committed Machiavelli's gospel to heart. She was a fascinating widow of dazzling person and captivating personality, as the world's eternal regard for her memory proves. Life should have been one triumphal procession for her, even in Scotland at that time, when the men in power had a negative attitude to all the things that she had been brought up to enjoy. She had one weakness, we are told by those who presume to set themselves up as judges in Israel; she was vehemently impulsive in love, whoever was lucky, or unlucky enough to be the object of it.

Exactly a year before her arrival in Leith, it had been instantaneously made illegal, by an Act of Parliament, for any Scot to belong to the Church of Rome. This Act, which appeared to have a religious motive, was based to a large extent on politics, and was intended to put a stop to the increasing power of France in Scotland. A powerful factor in pushing the Act through was the mode of life of the bishops and abbots who formed one of the 'Three Estates' of Scotland. They formed morganatic marriages, and less respectable unions, with the daughters of many Scottish gentlemen, and, when the numerous progeny grew up, they placed them in profitable and influential offices. In some notorious cases, as in that of Cardinal Beaton of St. Andrews, a host of mistresses, collected from all parts of Fife, 'from all the confines of the Horestii', was maintained in a species of seraglio.

As a Catholic, Mary was in a delicate, almost impossible position, because of this Act proscribing her religion, as well as being aimed at the expulsion of her late subjects, the French.

She agreed to support the Parliament and the Lords of the Congregation (amongst whom Argyll was prominent), and of whom Burton says 'a set of men wilder and rougher and more devoted to gross and secular objects is not easily to be found in history.' Even Knox and his ministers were powerless to restrain the greed and cruelty of these nobles. But Mary refused to give a retrospective Royal Assent to the Act of 1560, and she did not view with enthusiasm the persecution of her Catholic subjects.

At this juncture the Catholic Earl of Huntly, leader of the powerful and restless Gordon clan in the North-East, rebelled and gathered all the Catholic clans about him, of whom the MacGregors were still one of the most numerous and warlike, no doubt irritated by the pressure they were under. Mary was between the horns of a dilemma, a mythological beast that even Machiavelli had trouble with. She chose the lesser evil and decided to subdue Huntly rather than to have her sovereignty undermined. The Stuarts did not merely reign, they ruled.

The Reformation was probably never understood by the remote Highlanders, many of who had never even grasped the principles of Christianity: being conservative in all things, even had they comprehended Calvin or Knox, they would not have supported their ideas. They fought fiercely, as usual, but the Royal Army, led by Mary's bastard brother, the Earl of Moray, put down the rising with much bloodshed. He was not the 'Bonnie Earl' of the ballad, but his predecessor, later to be the Regent Moray, who, like his namesake, was also murdered. Despite the pathetic ballad on the Bonnie Earl's decease, which accuses Huntly (who had every reason to commit the manslaughter) there were not many in the Hielands or the Lawlands that shed a tear. Certainly not the MacGregors.

They had played a prominent part in the abortive rising; their leaders perhaps thought that Mary would never wage war with her co-religionists. But they could not suspect, unaware of the depths of Mary's character, that religious consideration was of secondary importance in her polity. Huntly's clans had challenged her royal authority; they had to be taught a severe lesson, the more effective as a general warning, *because* they were Catholics. The MacGregors should have hearkened to the old proverb, 'Meddle not with the Deil and the laird's bairns'. (Mary, stationed at Inverness, saw to it that Huntly was 'untopped'.)

After the short war was over, Argyll was waiting for them on the sidelines. But the rebels had still to be dealt with by law. An Act of Privy Council at Stirling, 22nd September, 1563, granted a Commission to the most powerful nobles and chiefs of clans to pursue Clan Gregor with fire and sword. In the same year, as if on a special request from him, to enable him to grind his own axe, Sir John Campbell of Glen Orchy was given similar powers, and all lieges were forbidden to help Clan Gregor in any way with food, drink, weapons, shelter, care for the sick, or transport.

The Privy Council was evidently in a humour to make a clean sweep of all kinds of evil-doing, for the first 'Act Anent Witch-craft' was also passed in 1563. The Bull of Innocent VIII entitled *Summis Desiderantis*, in 1484, had given papal authority to witch-hunting for the first time. One would have thought that the first act of the Protestants would have been to do the opposite, but the two centuries, almost, of torture and death for thousands of humble, as well as exalted Scots like Lady Bowes-Lyon, an ancestress of the Queen Mother, shows the savage nature that lay beneath their hypocritical piety. This persecution was paralleled only by the sufferings of the Clan Gregor over the same period.

The Campbell lairds were now Protestants, and the MacGregors were therefore not only rebels but heretics, and so outlawed by God and Caesar. They had acted most unwisely and were now at the mercy of their most inveterate foe, backed by the Lords of the Congregation, already described. To give the devil his due, the adoption of the Calvinist faith was not a sudden conversion, directed by expediency, on the part of the Campbell lairds.

In the Chronicle of Fortingal, Sir James MacGregor, Dean of Lismore, puts on record, in 1550, the death of Campbell, the first laird of Glen Lyon, and adds the remark that he regretted that this worthy man should have joined the sect of the heretics, that is, turned Protestant. It seems to have been a matter of genuine conviction, not policy, with the Glen Lyon laird, for he and his people were renowned for hospitality, and were in many respects opposite in character to the Glen Orchy line. It is one of the gravest misfortunes in Highland history that Robert Campbell of Glen Lyon, a century and a half later, should have led the Argyll company of soldiers in the much publicised Massacre of Glen Coe. There is little question that he had every reason to seek retribution from the MacDonalds, or MacIans, of Glen Coe. In a daylight foray in October 1689, when the Highlands were in disruption owing to Claverhouse's revolt in favour of the Stuarts, the MacIans and kindred bands, probably MacGregors and Stewarts, swept Glen Lyon completely bare, taking every head of cattle, horses, sheep, even down to the kitchen utensils from Campbell's house, leaving him ruined. This destitution forced him to earn a living by taking a commission in the Argyll Regiment. It is enlightening to consult the roll-call of the company he commanded. It shows only the leader and seven others were Campbells, the rest being of miscellaneous surnames, not all Highland, such as Scott, MacCallum etc. Many of them must, on evidence, have acted very unwillingly, giving obscure warnings, but all were under the severe military discipline of that age, when death was the punishment for desertion, disobedience, mutiny or even murmuring against orders.

To return to the MacGregors, they were not in the least intimidated by the Commissions of fire and sword in 1563, as they soon showed by their bloodily assertive deeds.

It is quite likely that Mary secretly admired their audacity and vigour, for we know that (despite the protestations of the godly) she gave her susceptible heart to Bothwell, a bold and desperate ruffian. She herself had absolutely no fear. She had proved this before she came to Scotland, when she was a freshly bereaved teenager, by earning the undying hatred of her mother-in-law, Catherine de Medici, the most dangerous vixen in Europe, who had her private poisoner, described for decency's sake as a 'Confectioner', who helped her victims to a premature demise. The Medicis had made their wealth in commerce, unlike most of the other noble families of Europe, who had grown rich by rapine and open war. Mary had already aroused the jealousy of Catherine by superseding her as the court beauty of France, lauded by the finest poets of the age; she now drove the Medici to white-hot fury by nicknaming her 'Fille de Marchand', the Shopkeeper's Daughter. The wonder is that Mary was not induced to partake of some choice sweetmeats. As I shall tell shortly, she took the MacGregors' part as often as policy allowed.

Chapter 4. The MacGregors' Mocking, Mayhem and Murder.

To show the reputation that the Clan Gregor had fully earned by Queen Mary's time, we must go back to the effect on them of the Act of 1488, aimed at destroying many of them, but failing in its purpose and, instead, rousing them to greater acts of violence.

As we know, on John of Glen Orchy's death Colin Campbell soon took the title of that territory. But this transaction was far from acceptable to Duncan MacGregor (Laudosach) of Ardchoille, as he soon showed by openly claiming that, as a successor to John, and tutor or guardian of Gregor MacGregor, a descendant (who had apparently been disregarded in the takeover), he was titular chief of Glen Orchy and would take it back by the sword.

He defied as invalid the Royal Proclamation (against the Clan Gregor and in favour of the feudal land grabbers). Without doubt it had been engineered by Campbell, Stewart and others. James III was assassinated in 1488, after fleeing from the battle of Sauchieburn, in the civil war instigated by the nobles who pretended to be acting for James IV, a minor. There was no effective ruler; a 'Royal Proclamation' was a farce. Duncan Laudosach laughed at it, and his mocking, mayhem and murder, as well as accompanying 'spreaghs' and 'tuilzies', may be read in every detail, grim, gay, and gory, to this very day in the 'Black Book of Taymouth' in a long narrative poem in Scots, 'The Testament of Duncan Laideus'. It was written from a narrative by a MacGregor, a curate of Fortingal, which is in the district of Appin, close to the abthanerie of Dull, and the piping-school of Drumcharaig maintained then by the MacGregors. Duncan was a contemporary of the recorder, so it is a first-hand account by a daring outlaw, and therefore not a story very common in literature, where such picaresque narratives are usually fictitious.

We have space only for an outline of the wild, devil-may-care deeds of Duncan and his successors of the early 16th century, but they are typical of the MacGregor spirit throughout the whole of their troubled history, where discretion and reverence were outweighed by foolhardiness and scoffing, which naturally did not improve the public image of these outlaws. Rob Roy carried the same wild spirit well into modern times.

Duncan and his merry men were hunted into Lochaber, where they lived dangerously for a time until driven by the Earl of Argyll back into the south, where they fell into the clutches of Glen Orchy. Duncan was jailed, as I mentioned in Chapter 8 above. He was chained like a wild beast in an underground pit, where food was thrown down to him in his captor's moments of relenting. As for his bed and sanitation, we had better not investigate. But before he was hauled up to the barbarities of being 'heidit' (for mercy was not on the cards), the monarch, James IV, called up all his levies and set off to the gathering-place deep in the recesses of the Lammermoors at Ellemford, whence they marched to Flodden, by way of numerous calls at Border castles, which gave the English time to put an end to this chivalrous and frivolous monarch and ten thousand of his countrymen. Campbell of Glen Orchy, and Argyll with nearly all the chief Scots 'deit valiently' with James and the Flowers o' the Forest. Duncan was not one of the chief mourners. He says in the poem,

> 'This heard I all, lying in deep dungeon.
> I thought me then half out of my prison.'

He escaped, and began afresh a long career of slaughter and rapine on those who had cheated him of his birthright. For many years he was an Esau, levying toll on all his enemy's flocks and herds. Now came the untimely death of James V, after another disgraceful exhibition of military ineptitude at Solway Moss had been conveyed to him at the same hour as the delivery of an unwelcome female child. These events threw Scotland again into anarchy. Duncan seized the occasion to take revenge on the MacLarens in Balquhidder, slaughtering twenty-seven men in one day.

Some years before this the Clan Donnachie, or Robertsons, had annoyed Duncan by supporting the Earl of Atholl in harrying those MacGregors who had found a primeval paradise in the labyrinth of the great Black Wood of Rannoch, a relic of the Caledonian Forest of prehistory. The Earl had captured and beheaded Alastair Dhu MacGregor. But although fourteen years had passed, Alasdair's debt was repaid in 1545, when Duncan, supported by another Alastair, of Glenstrae, took a very exacting toll of Clan Donnachie.

One day he heard, by a spy, that Campbell of Glen Orchy, the son of him who had prepared to behead him, was about to visit his kinsman, Red Duncan Campbell of the Hospitality, in Glen Lyon. Laudosach mounted an expedition to go by night to capture all the Glen Orchy dynasty. The Gaelic proverb says 'Night orders are not good'. Something went wrong with the staff-work and the plan miscarried. As Duncan relates it laconically and ruefully,

'The brig brak and we fell in the mire.'

Five years later, by which time Duncan MacGregor was no chicken, well into his sixties, he heard that a MacGregor had become a henchman of Glen Orchy. This turncoat had to be shown very firmly the error of his ways. In November, when there was very little daylight, even on a clear day, Duncan and his son Gregor set off for Alastair Owir MacGregor's house, broke in, and slew him, took his purse with £40 (Scots), equal to £2 (English), but a large sum then. When an unfortunate interrupter of this deed of hamesucken (or housebreaking) tried to intercept the MacGregor marauders, they 'strak his heid from his body.'

By the usual method, perfidy, Glen Orchy laid hold of Duncan and two of his sons, Gregor and Malcolm and beheaded them all on 16th June, 1552, the day devoted to St. Ciricius or St. Gregory. He perhaps chose this day with deliberate cynicism, as if challenging the patron saint of Clan Gregor to interfere and save them. He had recently turned Protestant and, although he was sure to remember all the holy days and to whom they were dedicated, he made a show of despising them. It is a pity another total eclipse did not intervene to save Duncan Laudosach a second time from imminent death.

Gregor MacGregor of Stronemelochan had been under the tutorship of Laudosach. He now became associated with Red Duncan Campbell of Glen Lyon and fell in love with his daughter. Campbell seems to have encouraged this match, but when MacGregor failed to collect the earthly benefits of it in the shape of an estate, he turned outlaw. With six score of wild catamountains of his clan he ravaged the Crown lands, returning by stealth from time to time to visit his bride. He was still prospering in this uncertain but exhilarating career when Queen Mary assumed the throne of her fathers.

She visited Inveraray in 1563 and began to put into practice her Machiavellian principles, or rather, the lack of them. She ran with the MacGregor hares and hunted with the Campbell hounds. She allowed the Campbells free quarters in the Royal castles and hunting-lodges when they were pursuing MacGregors. So hot did this chase become that many Clan Gregor men fled by ship to Ireland but, lest anyone should think that they had seen the last of them, they swore openly that 'when the nights grew lang' they would return and ravage the coasts of Argyll. Little doubt this threat caused many a sleepless night in Campbell and MacVicar households, when the winter waves roared from Machrihanish to Rhunahaorine and the rattling of the shutters could have been caused by some force more purposeful than the tempest.

Mary relented shortly after her Inveraray trip. She commanded Argyll to cease evicting the MacGregors and substituting them with Campbells, or his own henchmen of kindred clans. She also put a stop to the building of a tower of strength from which he hoped to conduct a campaign against the clan in Rannoch. The fact that he was building this on the Isle of Rannoch, *Eilean nam Faoileag*, Seagulls Island, near the west end of that great dreary loch, shows that he was so afraid of the MacGregors, Stewarts and Camerons that he dared not build it on the shore. No doubt he hoped to build galleys from which to menace the denizens of the Black Wood. He was halted, but, after Mary's flight in 1568, he built his fort and imprisoned MacGregors in it.

Turning to Menzies, another enemy of the MacGregors who had included a part of their territory in one of his title-deeds, but dared not enter it, Mary commanded him also, in no uncertain tone, to grant 'taks' of land to landless MacGregors. At least a part of her queenly heart sympathised with her persecuted co-religionists, undeserving though some of them were by reason of their irregularities. However, she began to blow cold upon them again on the following year, and Acts were passed by the Privy Council imposing penalties on those who helped MacGregors. She should have incurred a small fine herself, by law. The Earl of Argyll was picturesquely told to 'raise the shout against Clan Gregor and pursue them with fire and sword.'

In 1565 the blood-feud increased in violence. The famous Dean of Lismore, which is a large area stretching from Loch Tay as far as the Firth of Lorne, was a very respected man. He and his brother Duncan were both poets, and between them they collected and wrote in phonetic Gaelic all the Ossianic poems they knew, as well as others. This Book of the Dean of Lismore is one of the treasures of Scottish Gaeldom. James, the Dean, had three sons; Gregor was his legitimate son, while Dougal and a second Gregor were 'natural' sons, to use a less harsh epithet. Dougal followed his father's calling and became in time Chancellor of Lismore. Gregor, the 'natural', got into some sort of imbroglio with a man of ill-repute named James MacGestalcar. A Gaelic-speaking friend of mine thought the name to be of Central European gipsy, or of Spanish or Italian, origin. In the 15th century it is known that a number of Italian foresters, from a mountainous area of Italy, came to Scotland by arrangement to engage in work in some of the extensive woods in the Highlands. I have searched in atlases to find an Italian place-name like Gestalcar, but in vain. However, in reading Dante, I came upon the name Castrocaro, or Castellocaro, a small fortified village in Romagna, described in *Purgatory* as, 'Castrocara bad and Conio worse'. Though this is not conclusive it seems to give some grounds for a hypothesis that this evildoer MacGestalcar was descended from one of these Italian foresters, as he is called in the records 'the son of a forester'. Castlecary in Stirlingshire is, coincidentally, an old Roman fort, but I do not connect MacGestalcar with it.

With accomplices he stealthily surrounded the house where Gregor MacGregor and a young friend, Robert MacGregor, were asleep. Heaping up brushwood, they set fire to the house and when the young men rushed out, they slew them, defenceless as they were. Both were buried in the same grave at the end of the old Kirk of Kenmore (then named Balloch), to the great sorrow of the Dean and all the community.

Such an unnaturally wicked deed aroused Queen Mary to make a unique enactment. She ordered that Patrick Mac-Gregor and about a dozen other clansmen should be released from a bond of surety, or restraint on their behaviour, so that they could form a posse to bring the murderer to book. How surely and swiftly this was done may be read in the Chronicles of Fortingal for 27th July, 1565: 'James Mac-Gestalcar killed with his accomplices by Gregor MacGregor of Stronemelochan.'

Gregor survived for only four years, being relentlessly pursued by Campbell of Lawers and his minions. Tradition tells that he was the hero of the famous exploit still commemorated in 'MacGregor's Leap' over a lynn or waterfall, in Glen Lyon. His only way of escape from the Campbells, who had encompassed him when he was visiting his wife in Red Duncan's house, was by steeling himself to risk a fall into the thundering torrent; otherwise he faced a certain ignominious death on the heading block at Balloch. But that fate was not long delayed, for his royal protectress fled to England in 1568, to the tender mercies of the Virgin Queen who turned out to be a Virago. On 7th April 1570, after being, like his tutor, Duncan Laudosach, confined in a dungeon for a year, he was 'heidit at Balloch'. He was however, fully avenged that summer. The records for 22nd

August, 1570, relate with grim satisfaction, 'John MacCoul Dow slain beside Glen Falloch and 13 of Glenurchy's men slain that day by Clan Gregor.'

Gregor's son, Alastair MacGregor of Glen Strae, afterwards to be known as the 'Arrow of Glenlyon' (whose story may be read in all its true circumstances in a book of that title by A. A. Ramsay) was a child of seven when his father was beheaded. Alastair's own life-story forms the climax of this series of chapters of turmoil and bloodshed. He could not be expected to hold back his clansmen when they got an opportunity to pay back their long blood-debt. Compared with this feuding in the South-West Highlands, close to Glasgow and Stirling, even the infamous vendettas of Sicily look rather pale.

Chapter 5. Jacobean Genocide.

Mary's son James early showed he was a highly unstable mixture of statesman, assassin and buffoon. There has always been a nagging doubt that he was not her son, and certainly his placid acceptance of her execution does not seem an act of filial affection. In 1830 an infant's skeleton was found by workmen, walled up in Edinburgh Castle near the apartment where Mary was lying in. A scrap of cloth with the letters I. R. was around the skeleton, the I and J being identical then. Rumour, often a lying wench, whispered that a bastard of the Earl of Moray was substituted for Mary's child by Darnley, which was still-born. James certainly acted like a Stuart whoever his father or mother were. When he eventually ended his long minority, having tholed the insults and humiliations put on him by the nobles, he took over from the Regents and decided, in Stuart fashion, to deal with all those who had defied him.

As Professor Gillies puts it, in his *Hebridean in Goethe's Weimar*, speaking of James' schemes to colonise Lewis with Fifers, 'he pursued a policy of genocide in the Highlands and

Islands', where, of course, his chief agent was the Earl of Argyll.

Agnes Mure MacKenzie remarks, in her *Study of Scotland*, 'Unfortunately he tried the heavy hand by making an example of the MacGregors. They were a small clan on the Highland Line, beside the Campbells, which meant that the latter had ousted them from their lands. Being hot fighting stuff they proceeded to live by raiding their neighbours.' This is too vague a statement to have much bearing on Jacobean policy. The MacGregors had been forced for two centuries to live by pillage, before James appeared.

The MacGregors were not the only objects of James' blood-lust. The three Lewis expeditions met with disaster in the end, and the barbarous Lewismen decapitated the Gentlemen Adventurers and sent their salted heads back to James, packed in barrels. In revenge James encouraged Kintail to conquer Lewis for the MacKenzies, which was done with gusto.

Argyll, given a free hand, imprisoned MacLean of Duart and MacDonald of Sleat, in 1578, and continued his harassment of the MacGregors. He now discovered a new way of securing auxiliaries, for no cost, to slaughter the Clan Gregor. It was really a very ancient technique brought up to date. The details of it are to be read in a document unique in the annals of Scots law, though there are many examples of this kind of blood-rent in European feuds.

This document is entitled 'Donald and Dugald MacTarlich's Band', or Bond. Tarlich is pronounced Chairlie. It is rather long and repetitious, being in old Scots legal prose, so I shall omit it here.

The old adage, 'Give a dog a bad name, then hang him', was applied to the MacGregors as it has been applied through all history to groups of people accused of '*maleficium*', or dealing with Satan, whether they were heretics, gipsies, Jews, witches or wild Hielandmen.

I quote two parallel passages, the first from MacTarlich's Band, the second from a typical incitement to start a crusade against the Albigensian heretics of Languedoc. Each was an attempt to reach the 'Final Solution'.

From 'MacTarlich's Band', 1588.

> 'Understanding the clangregour to be manifest malefactors and his Majesties declarit rebellis for sundry slauchteris ewill turnis and oppressions done be thay ... we bind us to enter into deidly feud wt the clangregoure ... and in making of slauchter upon thame ... both privilie and openly ... until the time that the said duncane campbell of glenurquhay find himself satisfiet and contentit wt ye slauchter we sall do ...'

The reward for this 'slauchter' was to have the 'tak', or rent, of three small 'parcels' of land, probably filched from 'clangregoure'.

From the Bull of Clement XI, 1703, attacking

> '... the hereticks of the Cevennes, those accursed Remainders of the Old Albigenses ... to exterminate this Rabble of Wretches who in all ages of the World have been equally odious to God, and to Caesar ...'

The reward for this extermination was something which even the laird of Glen Orchy could not give, a full remission of sins and an entrance to Paradise.

History does not record the fate of the brothers MacTarlich, but it is unlikely that they enjoyed their earthly 'tak' for long, after the clangregoure got to know the terms of their rent.

The persecutions continued with ever increasing rigour and were bound to come to another crisis.

In 1589, John Drummond of Drummond-ernich, Royal Forester of Glen Artney, the north side of which is still a deer-forest, came upon some MacGregors hunting deer on what they considered their own territory. It was in Glen Artney, according to records, that, in 878, Hugh MacKenneth, King of Picts and Scots, was slain by Gregor MacDungal. Anyway, without the formality of a trial, Drummond hanged the poaching MacGregors, a common enough punishment both in Scotland and England for breaking the severe forest and game laws. The Highlanders never acknowledged Game Laws and felt free to take fish, flesh or fowl in their own territories. A well-known Highland gentleman used to drive in a pony and trap, towards the end of last century, shooting grouse, in defiance of the laws, wherever he found them.

The MacGregor chief took Drummond's action as an affront to be paid back in full, even though the poachers were a band of 'broken' men, not under his control. With an ambushing band he captured Drummond, and, if tradition does not lie, he executed him by having his horse drag him at the gallop across a rough piece of forest. They then 'untopped' him, to use the sport-loving Queen Mary's favourite phrase, and sat his head on a table in his sister, Mrs. Stewart's house, to confront her on her arrival home. To add insult to injury they stuffed bread and cheese into Drummond's mouth.

They later carried the grisly trophy to the Kirk of Balquhidder, where each MacGregor in turn put his right hand on the head and swore to uphold the deed in defiance of King James and the Privy Council. This was an open challenge which invited destruction.

There are several versions of this wicked deed, which was all the more defiant and arrogant because, at the time of Drummond-ernich's death, he was engaged in a hunt for venison to grace King James VI's wedding feast for Princess Anne of Denmark. Some versions say Drummond's hand only was cut off, but in an indictment of the time, the clan were accused in these terms: Oct. 1589: 'They cuttit and aftuik his heid and ... in the Kirk of Balquhither they laid their hands upon his pow (head) and in ethnick (heathenish) and barbarous manner swore to defend the authors of the murder.'

Another 'crusade' was launched which went on merrily for three years and led among many other executions to the death of a MacGregor chieftain whose wife is thought to have composed one of the most intense love-songs in Gaelic literature and music, '*Griogal Cridhe*', over his headless corpse. The pipe lament '*Cumha Mhic Griogair Ruadh-shruth*' is on this theme.

The MacGregors were by law stripped of everything that humans regard as the necessities, food, drink, shelter, care of babes, aged and sick; or that Christians of whatever persuasion had always regarded as their right, whether within or without the law, namely the Sacraments of baptism, marriage and burial. All these were denied Clan Gregor, and, in addition, there were instituted deprivations and insults so brutal that beasts would not have been subjected to them. Women associating with MacGregor men were branded with hot irons and whipped naked through the burghs at the tail of a cart. Children were torn from their mothers and farmed out in batches to the mercy of keepers. These things were done by pious Scots upon their own countrymen, but the Highlanders in general were regarded by Lowland Scots as insensate animals, so little do otherwise decent men observe common humanity when differences of language, customs, politics and religion drive them out of their wits.

But necessity has laws which brook no interference from kings or parliaments. The MacGregors became more adept at eluding their persecutors and, well-versed in retaliatory 'spreaghs' and 'sundrie slaughteris', continued their defiance.

The 16th century drew to a close with every portent of an even more squally age to follow; and the auspices did not lie.

King James had faced anarchy ever since his coming-of-age in 1587. His mother was executed in that year, in February, one of the most shameful episodes in modern history. It undoubtedly rebounded upon the monarchs of Europe, setting precedent for subsequent 'untopping' of sovereigns by axe or guillotine. It was severely condemned even by the Protestant rulers of North Europe who had as much to fear from Mary's machinations as Elizabeth. James, conformable to Stuart polity, did nothing to prevent or avenge his mother's death, deciding, in a cynical way, that his succession to the English throne took precedence over natural feelings. He restrained the Scots from marching south. The country was in a state of unrest everywhere, and James had a psychotic fear of assassination. The Ruthvens, he alleged on trifling evidence, had tried to kidnap him so he set out to exterminate them; his real reason was their part in the Rizzio murder; witch-hunting filled his spare time as he awaited the demise of the Tudor virago, who refused to name an heir, though she knew it had to be James, against whom she nourished an unprovoked spite. James could not be blamed for failing to tolerate the MacGregors. He appointed Argyll Warden of the South-west Highlands, and on the strength of this new title he behaved with overweening conceit.

Chapter 6. Glen Fruin.

At the tail-end of the century, in the same spirit that induces Scots to clear all debts before Hogmanay, Argyll was paying off old scores with his own Campbell relatives, as well as with the wily old Aulay MacAulay of Ardincaple. But MacAulay escaped the assassin's dirk and reached London, to achieve a notable if undeserved longevity, and to be the forebear of Lord Macaulay, the historian, and other distinguished Victorians. No better success attended Argyll's attempt on the life of Campbell of Ardkinglass, a friend of Alastair MacGregor, the chief. The MacGregors and Campbells got on very well together as clansmen and there was some intermarriage between these clans, too; the Campbell lairds, particularly the Glen Orchy line, were the obstacles. Argyll now played a double game, inciting the MacGregors to harry the countryside, especially his own enemies, the Colquhouns, and then, when they had made these raids, encouraging the Privy Council to attack them with fire and sword.

The Privy Council did not trust Argyll, yet, to get rid of the whole tiresome business, they gave him a new commission to deal with the clan. In a small letter clause one may still read the remarkable proviso that neither Council nor King would have the right to interfere and grant mercy to any MacGregor condemned by him. This arrogant act came out when the Commission was scrutinised, and the sly insertion spotted. The Council were now antagonistic to him.

They summoned him to 'compear' before them. He ignored the order. He was declared a rebel, over which he lost no sleep. He was fined 20,000 merks (£1,100 sterling) but would not pay. The MacGregors saw in his rebellious behaviour a glorious chance to clean up the countryside. Alastair's men were starving, for the winter was long and severe, so, reluctantly, when the season was advanced, he let them raid the region. In the summer of 1602, being encouraged by Argyll, they attacked the Colqhouns, who for long had been 'a sair hair in his neck' and against whom the MacGregors had a long account to square because of two clansmen, hanged by the Laird of Luss for killing a sheep when they were starving. On 4th June they swept Glen Mulchan in broad daylight, driving off six score of cattle. Argyll took no action, so the MacGregors, deceived by his quiescence, raided Glen Finlas, stripping it bare and killing and wounding a few Colquhouns who interfered.

Now was the time for reaction, so Colquhoun, no doubt encouraged by Argyll, mounted a bloody spectacle in Stirling before James, to arouse the royal emotions where they were most susceptible. He had a horror of blood, due it was said, to his mother having been pregnant when her favourite, Davie Rizzio, was murdered. Actually, despite the common tradition, reliable witnesses testified she was in another part of Holyroodhouse when the murder took place, but she was as much shocked by the event as if she had seen it. In any case, the long procession of Colquhoun widows and orphans, weeping and wailing afresh, and bearing bloody shirts on long poles, sent James into ecstatic fury, so well was the show stage-managed. Reports of the time say that many of the 'widows', who had been hired to be 'saulies' or 'dregies', or funeral mutes, got roaring drunk on their fees, and had to be disciplined.

Colquhoun was granted a Commission to raise a force against the MacGregors, Argyll not being in favour for the moment, though his scheme was about to bear the desired bitter fruit.

It took some time to collect a punitive force, as many would-be warriors could scarcely be persuaded to take arms against such a sea of troubles as always accompanied a conflict with 'Clan Gregor of the pipes and routs'. By January 8th, 1603, however, the force set off. The Colquhoun men were backed by the Buchanans, and by horse and foot from Dumbarton town.

Meantime the MacGregors had got wind of this and had sent the fiery cross round the whole area, to summon Camerons of Rannoch and MacIans of Glencoe, all of whom were professors in the science of 'spreaghs' and well pleased to join the MacGregors in what seemed a profitable excursion. This motley crew numbered about four or five hundred. They were led by Callum MacGregor, son of Gregor Dow of Glengyle. They gathered about the skirts of Ben Lomond and ferried to Tarbet, thence to Arrochar, and down the trackless east side of Loch Long, unburdened by horse, wagons, artillery or soup-kitchens.

The forces, eight hundred under Colquhoun, met in Glen Fruin, which is a pretty bare open glen quite unsuitable for the ambush which the MacGregors are said to have laid. But, since the credit for this effective stratagem goes to Robert Aberach MacGregor as the conceiver of it, we must believe it happened.

It was all over in a few minutes and the slaughter of the Luss and Dumbarton men began, over a hundred being slain, amongst them an ancestor of Tobias Smollet the novelist. The MacGregors lost very few, but amongst these was Alastair's brother John.

Fifty years ago, the writer, Alasdair Alpin MacGregor, visited Glen Fruin and was amazed that none of the inhabitants knew anything about the battle, or the significance of the venerable ash-trees and the memorial stone which was rumoured to mark the slaughter of a group of divinity students who had come to witness the battle. Alasdair Alpin need not have been amazed. After two centuries of brainwashing the Scottish bairns of his day were full of dates of Augustine and Alfred, to the exclusion of scenes enacted at their own doorsteps.

The MacGregors were blamed for this great atrocity in defeating a force sent to destroy them, and were further accused of murdering forty poor naked (i.e. unarmed) prisoners. (They would not be unclothed in a January day in Glen Fruin.) The massacre of prisoners was uncommon; the pious Covenanters under Leslie looked upon it as a goodly work to shoot the poor Irish men and women after Philiphaugh. But the wild MacGregors, though readily blamed, were not responsible for this crime at Glen Fruin. Indeed the Chief remonstrated fiercely with the miscreant who was responsible.

In 1609 in 'Pitcairn's Trials', it is recorded that a MacIntuach of Glen Coe was accused of having murdered 'with his awin hands forty puir nakit persons at Glenfroon.' A warrant for his arrest, or its equivalent, was issued though there is no evidence of his punishment having been carried out.

In the flush of victory the MacGregors harried the Lennox, which comprised Dunbartonshire and parts of Renfrew and Stirling. Glasgow at that time, though having had a cathedral for centuries, was no more than a large village of 7,000 people, and unable to raise a force equal to the rampant Clan Gregor, even in numbers, let alone arms. In 1638, when the first General Assembly of the Church was held in Glasgow, the representatives were in such fear of bands of robbing MacGregors that they were escorted by companies of armed retainers, who turned the godly Assembly into an unseemly brawl.

Clan Gregor's arrogant mass rapine could not have happened at a worse moment in all history. King James was all packed up to go to London and was in no humour to enter his United Kingdom leaving a large area of Central Scotland a smoking desert. He now applied all the force and fury at his disposal against the 'limmers and malefactors', to destroy them off the face of the earth: his main target was Alastair, who was held responsible, though many MacGregors, such as

Robert Aberach, were too stiff-necked and violent to be under his control.

In a deed of treachery, (comparable to Wallace's betrayal by John of Menteith) Alastair's friend, Campbell of Ardkinglass, captured him, but could not hold him, for when being ferried over Loch Lomond he slipped overboard and escaped by swimming off in the dark. But later, on getting a solemn promise from Argyll that, if he surrendered with all his nearest male relatives, he would be escorted into England by the newly formed Royal Guard, Alastair decided to take the chance to interview James in London, face to face, and crave mercy for the Glen Fruin affair. But, as was said at the time, with scant justice to the Celtic sense of honour, 'Argyll kept a Hielandman's promise, fulfilling it to the letter, but breaking it in the spirit.' Alastair's party were escorted over the border at Berwick Bounds but brought back to Edinburgh to face a travesty of justice.

Alastair wrote an accusation, still extant, against Argyll, and exposed his perfidy, but the Court decided to misname this and called it a confession. After a mockery of a trial, where the picked jury consisted of MacGregor's enemies from Dumbarton and Argyll, in the same style as the trial of James Stewart for the Appin murder of which he was patently innocent, Alastair and his relatives were immediately taken and hanged in a blasphemous manner on a gigantic black crucifix erected against the West End of St. Giles Church. The chief was hanged in the centre, being honoured by his pin being an ell higher than those of his relations.

Edinburgh was the scene of many Gothic horrors but this was surely one of the worst, if only because Alastair claimed to be descended without interruption for a thousand years from Fergus, King of the Scots, a claim made by James himself, though much less authenticated. But a man who would not raise a finger to save his own mother was not likely to spare a blood-related nobleman, rather remotely tied to him, it is true, but still of regal blood.

This mills of God, however imperceptibly, grind exceeding small, and Alastair was ultimately more than avenged on both Argyll and James. James' second son, Charles I, died on the scaffold in 1649. Argyll's son and grandson also were executed publicly, the first in 1661, and the other in 1685, their bodies preserved at Newbattle and buried at Kilmun on the Holy Loch along with a third Earl in 1705, on a day of accumulated mourning.

The ghost of Gregory the Great, King of the Picts and Scots, or perhaps the ghostly presence of St. Ciricius, himself a martyr, seems, in the very end of the Chief's Line, to have drawn his avenging sword, if not his protecting aegis, over those who put their trust in the power of his name.

Lewis Spence was a poet in the Edinburgh of my youth, where people still remembered the barbarities and injustices of the past by spitting upon the 'Heart of Midlothian', a paved heart in the street which marked the old Tolbooth, exactly on the spot where Alastair of Glen Strae was executed. I followed the custom, ignoring the notice 'Please do not spit on the pavement'. Lewis Spence obviously was of our mind in his poem 'Capernaum', a verse of which applies here.

> If a' the bluid shed at thy Tron
>   Embro, Embro,
> If a' the bluid shed at thy Tron
>   Were sped into a river
> It wad ca' the mills o' Bonnington
>   Embro, Embro,
> It wad ca' the mills o' Bonnington
>   For ever and for ever.

Part 3. Nameless.

Chapter 1. What's in a Name?

In 1597 Shakespeare asked this rhetorical question in *Romeo and Juliet*. In 1603, April, the MacGregors were asking the question again, but this time the answer was different. By an Act of Proscription in that month, only three months after Glen Fruin, the name of MacGregor was abolished; those who had taken part in the battle were all put under severe penalties, though the facts of the event show that the aggressors were the Buchanans, Colquhouns and Dumbarton men, who had set out to destroy the MacGregors and had themselves been destroyed. To the Clan Gregor the name meant a great deal, and it was obvious to the Privy Council that the name was so precious to the clan that the banning of it would be an ultimate step in the long process of exterminating them. They were ordered to take the names of any clan other than their own and to join these clans and obey their new chief. In many cases they were told which clans they were to adhere to. Many of them absolutely refused to change their ancient and honourable name, and continued openly to use the name Gregor or MacGregor. They were vigorously persecuted and put to death for their obduracy. No one ever knew how many of these defiant clansmen and their women and children were pursued, often with Campbells' bloodhounds, and buried like beasts in unmarked lairs among their native heaths. The much publicised massacre of Glen Coe was a very trifling incident compared with the Campbells' massacre of the MacGregors, and later, of the Lamonts of Cowal in the earlier part of the 17th century. Such

MacGregors as did adopt the names Stewart, Drummond, Graham, Campbell, or Buchanan, continued to be as adhesive as ever, but not to the clans of their forced adoption: whatever name they went by in daylight, or in public places, they always reverted to their true name when unobserved, or when about to gather for a retaliation on their foes. In short, the deprivation of their name made them more conscious of it, and the Act was, to end this paragraph as we began, what Shakespeare called 'a tale told by an idiot, full of sound and fury, signifying nothing'.

The surname of the clan was only one means of identifying its members. Within the clan the individuals had other names, as I said earlier, by which they were known, back through several generations. It is of some interest and relevance at this point, since the subject is names, to look at the Christian names favoured by the Clan Gregor in olden times, up to about the age of Rob Roy, end of the 17th century.

Conformably to their monastic or church origin, which I referred to in Part 1, when they grew up as a clan in the Glen Dochart area, most of the Christian names of the MacGregors were just that. Three of their most used names were of Jesus' disciples. These were usually given Gaelic forms. They were James or Seumas; John or Eoin, Iain; Andrew or Aindrea.

The Biblical name Daniel or Donald, Domhnull, was also a favourite. The name of the Christian martyr Ciricius or Gregor (Giric), besides being the clan name, was also a very favourite first name.

Patrick or Padruig was also of saintly origin.

Alexander or Alastair, Alasdair, was from the famous conqueror and was also the name of three Scottish kings of the post-MacBeth period. Robert, originally of French or Norman origin, was Gaelicised to Raibeart but usually shortened to Rob or Robin. A Norse name Ronald or Ranald was given by Rob Roy to one of his sons; Coll or Colla was another from the Irish Gaelic, as used in the name Finn MacCoul or Fionn MacColla, a pseudonym used by the late Tom MacDonald, the Scottish novelist.

The purely Gaelic first names are fewer in number. They are Malcolm or Calum, a votary of St. Columba or Colum; Dougal or Dugald, Dughall; Duncan or Donnachadh; Gillecolm, very rare, servant of Columba.

The extraordinary discovery is, that although Gregor was by all authentic accounts a Pict, and the clan (but not the old line of chiefs) are of Pictish origin, they never used Pictish personal names in olden times. Such names are Alpin or Ailpein, meaning of the high hills; Kenneth or Coinneach, Kinoid etc; Angus or Aonghas; Brude, Wroid, Bili, Drust; and they seem to have found such fascinating names as Canatulachama, Bliesblituth and Usconbuts quite resistable.

Modern MacGregors have been induced by the myths of origins to take the names Alpin, Kenneth etc. I think some fond father should do his proper Pictish thing and try out Guididgaedbrecach.

Amongst the Campbells the favourite names, which never seemed to vary in the Glen Orchy branch, were Colin and Duncan. The first of these names was avoided by the MacGregors.

We see, then, that the Proscription of the name MacGregor was nugatory, as long as the clan bore the traditional first names, or the name of their fathers. After the first burst of Council spleen the name was openly used in many parts of the country, and in return for their services in the cause of his family, Charles II, on his restoration in 1661, restored the full use of the name. Cromwell, during his term of influence in Scotland from 1650 to his death had established a very just if harsh regime in the Highlands, and there was no proscription then either. After over thirty years, at least, of full use of the name, a severe proscription was again put on it, in 1693 by William of Orange, at the instigation of the Earl of Stair, a Campbell nobleman who was also behind the atrocity of Glencoe. In due course I shall deal with the last restoration of the name about two centuries ago, which I remarked about in my Introduction.

Chapter 2. Choosing a New Leader.

Alastair of Glen Strae was executed nearly a year after the Acts proscribing the name, and his very exalted retribution, with his relatives beneath him, was meant to be a deterrent to his clan. This shows how little the Scots rulers understood the nature of the Glen Dochart people, and more markedly, of the Clan Gregor, for they existed, if not as a very united body, at least as a number of bodies that, like beads of mercury, coalesced at the slightest disturbance of their equilibrium. With some clans the obliteration of a common leader and still more, of a whole line, would have made it easier to extirpate them, or disperse them effectively. But, as events proved, Alastair's death made little difference to the cohesiveness of his followers.

It is not difficult to understand the mentality of those who backed Argyll in picking on Alastair to be the scapegoat. He was accessible and also accepted responsibility for the misdeeds of Clan Gregor. He was honest and trusting and as such was ripe for betrayal by Argyll and, by implication, by James also. Although James Stuart has his strong supporters (among them Isaac D'Israeli, student of Jacobean history in all its oddities), he was nevertheless a Judas on many occasions. He could slobber over and protest his kindheartedness to a favourite whom he was sending to exile and death. He sent a hired assassin into Poland to do away with a poor Polish gentleman named Stercovius who had found Edinburgh stinking and published this indisputable news in Latin, to spread the city's dunginess abroad. He found fault with an Oxford Scottish student, Ross, who had pinned up in very good Latin a thesis on the theme, 'All Scots go home except James'; had got him tried in Edinburgh because he knew the English would have treated it as a jolly good joke with a lot of point to it. The poor lad, a Perth gentleman's son, was hanged and his right hand and head stuck on spikes above the Netherbow Port. The theses of Thomas Ross and Stercovius were never found.

Hugo Arnot, an Edinburgh legal character, remarked in his *Records of Scottish Trials*, in 1785, that most of the trials during the reigns of the later Stuart kings were conducted, in Scotland, 'without the smallest regard for the principles of law and justice.' Alastair MacGregor had little hope of fair play.

But reliable records show that it was Robert Aberach MacGregor (i.e. of Lochaber) who, as I said earlier, worked out the blueprint of the Glen Fruin affray, and it was Callum of Glengyle who led the force. In a record of the Privy Council, Callum is accused of 'heiding his tribe at Glenfroon'. Perhaps each of the four or more MacGregor tribes was led by their own chieftains, though Alastair was the more prestigious.

It seems from the evidence that Alastair was picked upon 'to encourage the others.' For several years following the Edinburgh mockery, prominent MacGregors were at the mercy of the law but were not executed, though they were punished in various ways short of death. But the first act of the clan was to set up a new leader from one of the prominent land-holding branches, even if their tenure of the land, (perhaps, like Craig Royston, a few craggy bens and glens), was precarious or indeed disputable. Soon they were back at their only means of support – spreaghs and reivings. By 1633, James, having been gathered into the bosom of Abraham, or perhaps Airbertach, and having gone to the long home of Fergus the Long of Dalriada, the MacGregors were proving to be so viable that, as Scott says, 'They had broken out again in the counties of Perth, Stirling, Clackmannan, Monteith, Lennox, Angus and Mearns ... so commissions were again granted for enforcing the laws against that wicked and rebellious race.'

This argues that the MacGregors were very prolific, because, in the face of continual slaughter and deprivation, their numbers increased, not in a small area but over a large part of Central Scotland. Some of these counties, Angus and Mearns for example, are not mountain recesses, but are largely arable. I have particular records of some MacGregor families of this period, and they seem to follow the uneven pattern of procreation at that age, before what the Popes call the crime of Neo-Onanism (i.e. birth-control). Many MacGregor men left no successors, others left families of nearly twenty. Rob Roy's sons may be taken as a fair sample of 18th-century patterns. Coll had 14 children, James 13, Ranald 3 and Robin Og none (or perhaps only a natural son or two, attributed on slight grounds).

The nice question arises, were they promiscuous? One can scarcely allow a mere bagatelle like that to stand in one's way, when extermination is pressing. The Celtic marriage laws and customs were not uncontrolled. Like most primitive societies their taboos were much stricter on sex than those of our modern world. This does not mean that they were monogamous, which is a custom after all, not a law of God. In many areas in the Highlands, such as Upper Strathspey, even into the 18th century, trial marriages were customary. They were to last for a year and a day. If, at the end of that term, the report was satisfactory, they continued as fully articled man and wife; if not, they parted on more or less good terms. Any child born of an incompatible cohabitation was not condemned to bastardy: usually the woman took the child and was known as a grace, pronounced grass, widow. Her experience did not render her less liable to try again.

Perhaps the hard-pressed MacGregors reverted to the pre-Christian customs of their ancestors. They derived no benefit or protection from any laws of God or man. Why should they observe them? Before leaving this vital question may I quote an incident reported circumstantially by Dio Cassius, a Roman historian of the second and third centuries AD.

> 'The empress Julia Augusta taunted the wife of Argentocoxus, a Caledonian envoy in Rome, accusing the Caledonian women of copulating promiscuously with their husbands. To which the Britoness retorted, "We have, openly, intercourse with the best men; but you Roman women are polluted secretly in adultery with the worst men." So [spoke] this Britoness.'

Isabel Henderson, writing of the Picts, who shared Scotland with the Caledonians at that time, says there is no reliable record of Caledonian and Pictish marriage customs. The above passage, if it is not just Dio Cassius' way of having a crack at the Romans, (for he was born in Bithynia) seems to indicate polygamy, or polyandry, or marriages within a prescribed social group. But I do not believe the above story, for several reasons. The main reason is that the Romans did not come into contact with the Caledonians until about 80 AD. Julia Augusta, the daughter of Augustus Caesar, was by all accounts a notoriously loose woman, who in turn married three prominent Romans, the last being Tiberius, a licentious emperor. She was dead long before Agricola encountered the Caledonians. Dio must have heard rumours about the Caledonian marriage habits, quite unreliable. In the same misty region, the Caledonian Forest, is found, growing vigorously, the tall tale that Pontius Pilate was a native of Fortingal. He had died near Grenoble before the Romans even began their long conquest of Britain in 43 AD.

I apologise for these small digressions, but at least they are a comic relief from the weary repetition of persecutions of the Clan Gregor. Their fecundity was not exceptional, for they were subject to the same natural laws of gestation as all other humans. They did not take fertility drugs, and bring forth, like coneys among the rocks, in batches. They loved their children, often to distraction, the more so because they were bringing them into the world like fox cubs, or badger pups, to be hunted as feral beasts by merciless fellow-Scots.

Although treated no better than the beasts that perish, the clan was very well versed in all the genealogies back as far as the beginning of the land-robbing.

The most outstanding MacGregor of the 16th century had been Dougal Keir, Dougal the Dusky or Dun-skinned, son of Gregor, and grandson of John of Glenorchy, the last laird, who died in 1390. His was a formidable reputation. Many years after his death, which must have occurred at the latest in the first half of the 16th century, he, or his very active ghost, was being blamed for atrocities such as that at Glen Fruin, already described. His reputed gravestone, 'The Grey Stone of MacGregor', was in Fortingal Churchyard. Sir Walter Scott says that when it was proposed by some vandals to convert it into a lintel, or doorstep, or other domestic purpose, a very formidable MacGregor of fanatical nature, which combined very explosively with feeble-mindedness, stood on the stone, swinging a broad-axe and threatened to brain the first to desecrate his ancestor's tomb. It was not molested.

Dougal's younger son Gregor got a lease of Glen Gyle from the laird of Buchanan, but died in the prime of life, possibly by violence. Dougal's older son Callum led the clan at Glen Fruin. The exploits of his life would fill a volume or two. One or two incidents will perhaps serve.

He attempted to carry off an heiress, a relative of the Earl of Argyll, during the severe proscription about 1610. The Earl tried hard to catch him. Knowing he often frequented a public house above Balquhidder, he surrounded it with a band of his retainers. Callum not being inside, the Earl and his company went in for whisky, bread and cheese. Callum with a gillie arrived later and cautiously peered through the small window, unglazed, of course. He heard the Earl say he wished he had as firm a hold of 'Malcolm og MacGregor vic Dowgall Kier' as he had of the hunk of cheese he was grasping. Callum's gillie cocked his flintlock to shoot Argyll but Callum would not allow such a cowardly act. Later Callum wrote and told Argyll about it. To his great credit, the Earl obtained a pardon for Callum from the Privy Council.

Callum married, first, a MacFarlane lady, by whom he had two sons. He left her and married a MacDonald chief's daughter, who presented him with nine sons and daughters as well. There were therefore plenty of Glen Gyle claimants to Alastair of Glen Strae's vacancy, but according to Miss A. G. M. MacGregor's *History*, the Glen Gyle branch was only fourth in importance; they were 'also-rans' in the race for the Chief Stakes.

But whatever position was assigned to them in the punctilios of genealogy, they were not wanting in men of desperate deeds, and fully lived up to the clan motto which forms a complement to 'My race is royal'. It is 'E'en do and spare nocht'.

There is a hillock in Glen Ogle, that short but awesome glen that runs from Lochearnhead to Glen Dochart, which is named in Gaelic *Meall a Mhadaidh* (in English, the knoll of the dog). It is here that Callum was being pursued by the Campbells headed by a bloodhound. As the hound came belling over the summit of this rocky lump Callum, who was lying in wait, shot it with his long-barrelled flintlock. He was then able to make good his escape, knowing that the 'wry-mouths', however keen, could not pick up the scent. His gun is still preserved.

On another escapade he was hiding on an islet in Loch Katrine, probably of Portnellan, and Campbell's men were camped on the woody shore, quite a long way off, but near enough for voices to carry over the water, Callum had taken the precaution of sinking all the boats except the one he was using himself. Argyll, knowing the islet to be barren, thought that he would starve Callum into surrender, so he sat down with his men to await that event. One of the band, a soutar, or cobbler to trade, lit a fire to prepare some victuals. Callum, directed by the smoke, took his very good gun and shot the cobbler, killing him. As he fired he cried out the cryptic sentence, *'Thugad thall a chrom thruaill sloightear.'* (Get out of my way, you greasy crook!) In Gaelic a crook is also a cobbler, who is usually hunchbacked from bending over his work. The Argyll men were so astounded at the crack of the gun followed by the verbal crack, both hitting the bull's-eye, that they concluded Callum had the second sight. They set off hurriedly, never to return, and Callum lived to enjoy a peaceful old age in Glengyle.

I am indebted for these anecdotes to Mr. Andrew MacEwan, who drew my attention to them from an account by Mr. Donald MacGregor, dominie of Rossdow, in Miss A. G. M. MacGregor's *History*.

Whatever their relative position, the Glen Gyle branch had the consolation prize in the long run, which proved to be incomparably more glittering than any other. The grandson of Callum of Glen Gyle was no other than Rob Roy, to whose tumultuous career we shall return later.

One of the branches of the MacGregors, following the failure of the Glen Strae line, was that of Aberach, or Lochaber family. In the late 16th century their head was Duncan

Aberach MacGregor. He had two sons, Robert the elder and Padruig or Patrick, the younger. Robert masterminded Glen Fruin, after which he was a hunted man. Threatened men live long, however, and on August 26th, 1626, he was ordered by the Council 'to depart of this country ... to serve in his Majesty's [Charles I] wars beyond sea and never to be found again within any part of his Majesty's dominions in time coming under pain of death.' Notwithstanding this severe edict, he was in the Balquhidder area in 1631, with his younger brother Patrick, to patch up a long quarrel with the Buchanans. Not a whit reformed, he was charged on 19th January 1637, suspected of slaughtering 'Johne Stewart' on the previous Christmas Day. His sons Gregor and Duncan were true to their father's reputation and about the time of King Charles I's execution in 1649 they were indicted for horse-stealing, and conducting all sorts of such peccadilloes, with a few mayhems thrown in, on the Highland Line. Some of their descendants may have toted guns and been bad hombres in the Woolly West, for it is unlikely that the Aberachs could have settled down to a steady executive job in either hemisphere. 'They change their sky, not their spirit, who sail across the ocean,' observed Horace; and this restive race of the Lochaber MacGregors, though it has vanished out of the ken of genealogists, is pretty sure to be active yet.

I have no space to deal with, far less have I the desire to involve myself in, the intricacies of Clan Gregor genealogies. Absalom, fatuously proud of his great beard and hair, as well as of his royal ancestry, got himself entangled in the contorted branches of an oak tree in the wood of Ephraim, and was the easy target for the javelins of his adversaries. I should not wish to find myself in such a quandary, for assuredly that is the fate, metaphorically of course, of rash writers who meddle with the laird's bairns of Clan Gregor. Many people have assumed that this book was to be a record of my perambulations among the tombs and the tomes. I trust that I have been able to raise my sights a bit higher now and again.

There are many descendants of branches of Clan Gregor in all parts of the world who are very well versed in their own family trees, whether of the Roro, or Glen Lyon, branch, who suffered so severely from the savagery of Stewart, the Wolf of Badenoch, in mediaeval times. The Balhaldie co-laterals, whose head was elected clan Chief at a full gathering of all MacGregors in 1714, when there was a prospect of the Jacobite rising (of 1715) are also still extant, and fully aware of their descent, both here and in America. Other branches, too numerous to particularise, are not at all extinct, and rejoice in family memories of their fathers and mothers that begat them.

Chapter 3. 'Peace and Tranquillity at Home.'

Proscription in English sounds a fairly mild expression, like a little piece of paper one takes to the chemist to make up, for a tummy upset, or the like. In Gaelic it reads '*Dìteadh gu bàs*' or 'Condemnation to death'. The Proscriptive Acts of April 1603, drawn up in the white heat of the reaction to Glen Fruin, and the subsequent 'Herschip of Kippen', were as severe as could be legislated for; indeed they went far beyond any legal powers of Scotland, even though Scots law was to a large extent founded on Roman Law, not anything to be proud of, for it supported institutions like slavery, and torture to extract confession. Innumerable MacGregors were executed without even the pretence of a trial.

The pogrom was a Russian institution which was so christened in 1905, within my lifetime, when the liberal policies of the Tsar did an about-turn and the Cossacks were turned loose upon the proletariat in St. Petersburg. Although the Russian word is a neologism, it does not embody a new idea, nor was it intended, even in Russian, to be aimed mainly at Jews. The victims of it could be any group, gipsies, students, extreme religious groups like the Doukhobors. Pogrom in Gaelic is *Dìteadh gu bàs*; in English, proscription.

It was instituted in Scotland by the new monarch of Great Britain as the very first enactment, a week or two after he had assumed the throne of Elizabeth. The Privy Council appeared to be the legislators, but James never tolerated a bureaucracy to rule over Scotland; the Privy Council was his personal mouthpiece, and it was his personal antipathy to the Clan Gregor that he implemented by dragooning the Highlands. His measures were as severe as those levied by the Assyrians and Chaldeans upon the Semitic peoples, which forced them in the 6th century BC to flee westwards by sea to form colonies in North Africa and the Western Mediterranean. These ancient extirpators 'had no compassion upon young men and maidens, old men or him that stooped for age', but they were outdone in draconian measures by the Scots of the 17th century in the years of grace. Unlike the Semites, the MacGregors had no chance to escape en masse by sea, unless, as often happened, they were shipped as slaves to Ireland or to America. They had to betake themselves to the inaccessible fastnesses of Rannoch, the Trossachs or Rothiemurchus.

I use a quotation from the fulsome dedication of King James' version of the Bible for my ironical chapter heading, to show the opposite poles of conduct and sentiment between Southern England (where about two score of learned and pious men set about one of the noblest labours of the human intellect, from 1604 to 1611), and what was going on under the same personal direction in the Southern Scottish Highlands, at exactly the same time.

In 1610 and again in 1613, on Midsummer's Day, further Acts of Proscription, which one would have thought superfluous, were passed. Shakespeare was still alive, and perhaps King James had a Royal Command Performance of *Midsummer Night's Dream* at the Globe Theatre in 1613, little caring that hundreds of his Scottish subjects were being subjected to a Midsummer Night's Nightmare as they were hunted down by Argyll's bloodhounds.

Again in 1617, in Chapter 26 of the Acts of Council, a further set of proscriptions were put on the book, in language which seems almost to mirror the spluttering of legal quill-pens. Sir Walter Scott describes it in his 'big bow-wow' style: 'The Scottish Legislature, who apparently lost all the calmness of conscious dignity and security; and could not even name the outlawed clan without vituperation.'

By this time the MacGregors were all but destroyed, for the landholders, most of whom were clan chiefs, had now been made liable to heavy fines for harbouring the clan. Many of the proprietors were probably unaware that parties of clansmen and their families were sheltering in the pathless thickets and rocky labyrinths of their domains; more, no doubt, would let sleeping dogs lie, knowing the positive lust of the outlaws for repaying debts with compound interest; but some kindred clans, Grants and MacAulays, felt it incumbent on them to aid their blood-brothers.

The Laird of Grant was fined the crippling sum of 40,000 merks, or £26,666 Scots, or £2,222 English, for extending a helping hand. The Earl of Stair (Campbell) got a few thick slices of this bread that Grant cast upon the waters. All the same, as Ecclesiastes preached hopefully, the Grants 'found it after many days' in the very acceptable form of Rob Roy who, remembering the old generosity, turned up with a couple of hundred caterans, armed to the teeth, to help Patrick Grant gainst the threats of the MacIntoshes. But Rob was still in the teeming womb of time when the Proscriptions were at their height.

In this excruciating persecution the MacGregors suffered the same atrocities as are described in the starkest passage of the *Iliad*.

> *Nemo manas fugias vestras*
> *Non foetus gravida mater gestat in alvo*
> *Horrendum effugiat caedem.*

My rendering is:

> Let none escape from your clutches,
> Not even the mother whose belly is heavy with foetus
> May flee from the horror of the slaughter.

On the dial of human history we are only a few seconds farther on than this Jacobean genocide, and only a fraction of a second later than the Hitlerian and Hiroshima holocausts. I cannot ever, no more than can any of these modern survivors, forget this deliberate attempt to abort my existence, even though I should never have known of it, any more than the dozen generations that anteceded me. What countless hundreds of men and women, of spirit and genius, this 'high and mighty prince James, Defender of the Faith etc' deprived of being, can only be guessed at: a matter for sad conjecture, too, is the benefit these MacGregors and their putative descendants would have brought to their native land in every art, industry and social activity.

As my reader can see, I never view these events with levity, though I appreciate the grim humour in many incidents. In looking at life, as we all know, for those who feel, it is a tragedy, for those who philosophise, a comedy. 'Well at ease,' Carlyle said, 'are those for whom life is a shallow dream.'

Common humanity came at last to the aid of the MacGregors, and many Highlanders were loath to join in the head-hunting which was encouraged by the Privy Council. Any notorious criminal was able to purchase a pardon by bringing in a specified number of MacGregor heads, depending on the scale of his crimes. There are many traditional tales about this period, which would be very effectively recounted in all their gory details, over a flickering campfire in Glen Dochart or Rannoch or Glen Coe, as I used to tell them myself, in the velvety darkness of a summer night, to my captive audience fifty years ago. One such story relates how a miscreant, carrying a dripping sack of six innocent 'powes', began to feel a shade of remorse. The heads started to hold a whispered conversation which grew in volume to a torrent of maledictions, in which Gaelic is very rich. The headhunter began to run and stumble. At last he began to cry out against his accusers. His clamour was heard by a band of MacGregors who soon strung him up to a handy bough and buried the sack beneath him.

It has to be confessed that a Robert Aberach MacGregor, who, try as I may to avoid this conclusion, I can only identify as the planner of Glen Fruin already mentioned, was told that he would be able to purchase a pardon for his numerous hamesuckens (assaults on householders in their own homes), and herschips (robberies), in return for six MacGregor heads of as much value as his own. He was dissuaded from this thuggery by MacGregor threats to 'untop' him in turn. I have quoted earlier his deportation order, which was never obeyed. Some claims of chieftainship, or similar title, have been made on the basis of descent from Patrick Aberach, his brother, who was younger than Robert. It is easy to see why no self-respecting person should ever wish to claim descent from this unprincipled wretch, whose name deserves to be a hissing and a reproach for all time, linked of course with those who arranged this bestial transaction. The 'Head-hunting' Commissions had been issued in London in August 1610.

About this year, too, Argyll had been quaintly advised 'to lay mercy aside and by justice and the sword ruit out and extirpat all of that race.' The use of the word 'race', which in Gaelic is *sìol* or *clann*, is not our use of the word, which has come to have associations with unpleasant occurrences. It could well have meant merely a clan, or it could have denoted a recognisable kind of people, descendants of the old inhabitants of Perthshire.

Chapter 4. Changing Fortunes of War.

James VI and I died in bed, a 'fair straw death' as it was called, meaning unviolently, the first of his dynasty to achieve this peaceful end. Unluckily Henry Stuart, the gifted heir presumptive, did not live to be Henry the Ninth. Charles, who had in overflowing measure the family characteristic of pursuing a fixed idea of personal political supremacy, inherited his father's war on the MacGregors. In 1633 he passed the Proscriptive Act I mentioned earlier, to quell their uprising in several Scottish districts, with the usual effect: they continued to flourish.

The clan apparently forgave him to the extent of supporting him when the Great Civil War broke out. Scott says that they felt obliged to be Royalists because their ancestors had been kings of Scotland, but he doubts the sincerity of this protest. He suggests that the prospect of conducting justified raids on the Covenanting country, rich in flocks and herds, and less movable booty, was too attractive to resist.

In Scotland the Civil War became a war between the great rival families of Argyll, and Graham, Marquis of Montrose. The Highland clans, except the Campbells and their allies, ranged themselves behind Montrose. It was virtually a racial conflict between Highlanders and Lowlanders. The Mac-Gregors took a heavy revenge on their hereditary persecutors. At Kilsyth, as some records show, they were present at what was, in effect, a massacre of the Covenanters, who were trapped in a peat-bog and shot without mercy. Of the 41 men, for example, who were levied from Anstruther for the Covenanters, not one returned, and even at the beginning of the 19th century old people used to speak of relatives who marched against Montrose and were seen no more.

At Inverlochy, near Ben Nevis, after an astonishing crossing of Drumalban, the Spine of Britain, in the depths of a severe winter, which no regular troops could have endured, and in which the poet Ian Lom (the Bald) MacDonald took part, Montrose's clans fell on the Duke of Argyll and his forces and destroyed them. MacCailean Mhor, the Argyll himself, was forced to flee in his galley down Loch Linnhe. The victors had already devastated the whole of Argyll's country, burning Inveraray and Campbeltown. But all this internecine misery ended with no joy for the Scots, even if the MacGregors gave their libidos a break. Montrose was executed with savage exultations from the ministers, which not long after they no doubt repented of, when their interference with military science caused the massacre of the Covenanting army by Cromwell at 'Dunbar Drove'. In the unsuccessful rising of Glencairn in the Royalist Cause, 1653, the forces of Charles II gathered at 'MacGregor's Hall' on the Isle of Loch Rannoch.

Strangely enough both Cromwell and his successor on the Royalist side, Charles II, lifted the persecutions of Clan Gregor. The first, as I said in Part 3 Chap. 1, because of a policy of fair play and opposition to fanaticism; the second because the Macgregors had supported his father and himself, particularly in Glencairn's Rising in the Highlands. He was, however, only acting as a typical Stuart and paying off family debts. His dragoons were very active in the land of the Westland Whigs, in Ayrshire, Lanark and Galloway, where thousands were martyred in a quarter century of misrule. When the 'Highland Host' were quartered on families of the Covenanters after their unsuccessful risings, little doubt the MacGregors, MacDonalds and Stewarts would take part in the tyrannical act, enforcing a policy of 'Divide and Rule', which continued to split Scotland in two.

In 1661 the Clan Gregor had had the pleasure of hearing that Argyll's execution in Edinburgh had rid them of their chief persecutor. He was not charged with his campaign against the MacGregors, but, in addition to his treason against the Stuarts, which was arguable, he was accused on ample evidence of his betrayal, treachery, perjury and massacre of the Lamonts of Cowal, the remains of whose last defence post, Toward Castle, still stand to this day, although only as a ruined outline. Two hundred of the Lamonts, who surrendered under promise of being spared, were hanged or slaughtered, and the clan virtually wiped out. Once again Mercy was pushed aside.

These respites of persecution for the MacGregors were too good to last. After the English Revolution, Dutch William arrived from a land of tolerance, and the British expected magnanimity from him, both politically and in religion. His coming may have been a welcome change for England and the Presbyterian Scots, but it was far otherwise for the Episcopalians of North-East Scotland, and the Catholic clans of the Highlands. William's unfamiliarity with the English language, and his total ignorance of Scottish affairs, put his whetstone at the disposal of all those, like the Earl of Stair, who had axes to grind.

Stair's father, Argyll, had been executed in 1685, under the Stuarts. His son now got to work beneath the cloak of pacification and indemnification, to wreak vengeance on his personal foes among the clans. The outstanding objects of his spite were the MacIans of Glen Coe and the MacGregors, with all those clans that had taken part in the rout of Killiecrankie high up on his list.

The Glen Coe Massacre followed, outstandingly condemned, not so much on account of the slaughter of all ages and conditions, as because of the breach of the ancient law of hospitality, more binding than any of the ten commandments. Yet such was the impenetrable stupidity, or stubborn self-conceit, of William III, advised of course by Stair, that in the year *following* Glen Coe, severe Proscriptive Acts were again laid on the MacGregors. They had almost forgotten what it was to suffer, much less to evade persecution, and their tempers, never very well-controlled, were far from soothed or subdued by this new denunciation.

This much, however, may be fairly stated, to account for this fresh proscription, that Lieutenant-Colonel Donald Mac-Gregor, the father of Rob Roy, and, like him, a very turbulent spirit, had been one of the foremost leaders in the 1689 rising, and had led a hundred Glen Gyle MacGregors to follow 'Bonnie Dundee'. Had Dundee not been slain at Killiecrankie, Donald MacGregor would probably have been prominent in history. But he died in 1695, a death hastened by his long and severe imprisonment in Edinburgh Tolbooth, where he knew all the Gothic horrors of that den.

I am forced to connect this renewed persecution of the MacIans and MacGregors with the religious intolerance which characterised the Presbyterian ascendency. As many parish records show, this led to a tyranny imposed by the bigoted section of the Church of Scotland, which, especially in Glasgow and the whiggish counties like Ayrshire, was not abated even by Burns' day. Many people think that Burns' satires were fired at a wide religious target, but this is erroneous, He castigated the Associate Synod, strong in Ayrshire as well as in other areas, the two sects of which were the 'Auld Lichts' and the

'New Lichts' who had little difference in doctrine, but a common belief in the efficacy of hellfire. Although the MacGregors had been Catholics from olden times, Rob Roy was a Presbyterian for the middle part of his life, but as Scott observes wryly, he returned to the Catholic faith, finding, in its wider forgiveness and remission of sin, a religion more profitable to one of his calling. My own MacGregor ancestors belonged to the 'New Lichts', and believed in all the reality of the fire that is never extinguished.

Sir Thomas Urquhart, who flourished before this fanatical repression and whom I like to support in his magnanimous views, commented in these terms on the religious schism in Scotland.

> 'It is perceivable that all Scots are not Presbyterians, nor yet all Scots Papists, so would not I have the reputation of any learned man of the Scottish nation buried in oblivion because of his being of this or this or that or yon, or of that other religion ... which would prove absurd to a true cosmopolite.'

These words were written in the 17th century when Scots were hacking fellow-Scots to death crying 'Christ and no Quarter', and when the agents of James VI and I were hanging Jesuits, burning witches and head-hunting MacGregors. One would expect that the lapse of two and a half centuries should have led to an enlightened spirit, especially in Scotland, where progress of all sorts was boasted of in mid-Victorian days. It is therefore shocking to read in the *Imperial Gazetteer of Scotland* (1860) under the title 'Highlands', that some of our nation had so little progressed from barbarism and bigotry as to write these rancorous passages.

> 'This occasioned the whole district (the West Highlands) to send up rank and fetid crops of poisonous herbage from the manurings of Popery left upon its soil.'

> 'Throughout the 17th century Popery was allowed to run riot nearly at will in the Western Highlands ... and Episcopalianism, in the feeble and worthless form ... which characterised it in Scotland, maintained full possession (in the North-East).'

> 'The Established Church (in 1725) aided by the routing of Popish priests and of Jacobitical Episcopalian ministers, began to spread its roots.'

Sir Thomas Urquhart of Cromarty was a good European long before we 'joined Europe', and he would have been more at home in the company of Gregory MacDungal, who granted the gift of liberty to a rival church, than he would have been a thousand years later in the presence of the Reverend Marius Goring who edited the *Gazetteer*.

When Queen Anne died, and the 1715 rising came, the MacGregors were favourably disposed to aiding the Stuarts, but not with zest, for that family had been a mixed blessing. They had two other reasons for rising: they loved campaigning and they had no love for the Whigs. But Argyll was now becoming more acceptable for a personal reason which will soon appear.

Chapter 5. Rob Roy.

That turbulent warrior, Donald Glas (Grey or Pale) Mac-Gregor of Portnellan in Glen Gyle, whom I introduced in the previous chapter and dismissed temporarily (after deploring his death from maltreatment received in Edinburgh Tol-booth) was born in 1620, at the time of the worst pro-scriptions. He was named after his uncle Donald Glas MacDonald. He married Margaret Campbell who came of both Campbell of Glen Orchy and Campbell of Glen Lyon chiefs. When Campbell of Glen Orchy married the widow of the 6th Earl of Caithness and wished to take over his newly acquired Earldom, he was opposed by the Caithness Sinclairs. He raised a force of Campbells and was supported by Donald Glas MacGregor's eldest son John with a strong force of his clan from Glen Gyle. They marched to the neighbourhood of Wick, where, having crossed the Ord of Caithness, a mountain ridge, they met the Sinclairs, The mixed force of former clan rivals camped by the Altimarlach Burn, while the Sinclairs sat up all night drinking and carousing in Wick. 'Merry nichts mak dowie morns' was a proverb well illustrated. The wild charge of the Glen Gyle and Glen Orchy men resulted in such a slaughter of Sinclairs that the victors passed over the burn dryshod upon their corpses. The victors immediately set to, and, in a very successful liaison, composed the two pipe tunes 'The Campbells are Coming', and the 'Braes of Glen Orchy'. In Gaelic the first is '*Baile Inbhearaora*' or 'Inveraray Town'.

It is little wonder that, with such a strong Campbell background, Rob Roy, Donald's third son, should have taken the name Campbell when the proscriptions of 1693 came into effect.

In view of the doubts that are sometimes cast on the existence of Rob Roy in the flesh, here is a verbatim recording of his baptismal notice from the parish records of Buchanan, which adjoins Callander parish.

'On the 7 day of March 1671, Donald McGregor of Glengill pr of Callender upon testificat from the min^r yrof Margaret Campbell – son baptised Robert. Witness Mr. Wm Anderson minr and Johne McGregore.'

Very early in his career he was concerned in several notable exploits, the first of which was the famous Herschip or Harrying of Kippen when he emulated his predecessors of Glen Fruin, by driving off great numbers of sheep and cattle from that fertile strath west of Stirling. In another exploit, which was undertaken because of a higher urge than mere gain, he took a large body of Glen Gyle men to Strathspey; I have already mentioned this; I would like to fill in some colourful details.

Patrick Grant was a flamboyant chieftain of Strathspey who went about the Rothiemurchus area with a band of two dozen desperadoes executing summary and often quite unsubstantiated sentences on supposed wrongdoers. He was dressed in fine velvets, satins; his shoes lined with down and his cap adorned with great tail feathers of eagles. His table was furnished with choice meats and imported wines. He was what we should call now an ornament of the third sex.

He fell out with the MacIntoshes about 1690 over the supply of water to his mill. The chief of his rivals had built another mill farther up the burn, and was diverting the water for his own use. He now threatened to burn Grant's mill. In his extremity Grant sent hurriedly for Rob Roy, nearly a hundred miles off, by the tortuous paths through the Cairngorms.

Soon after, as the MacIntoshes sat menacingly on all the adjacent hillocks, Rob appeared, accompanied by a solitary piper. On being querulously asked by Grant where his 'tail' of the Clan Gregor was, Rob slapped him on the back and said, 'Cheer up, what though the purse be light in the morning, who can say how heavy it may be by nightfall?' He bade the piper blow a pibroch, 'The Rout of Glen Fruin', and as the notes swelled, bands of MacGregors sprang from the rocks and bushes, fully armed. As they appeared, the MacIntoshes disappeared in inverse ratio. The force of Grants and MacGregors then set fire to MacIntosh's mill, while the piper composed a new air to fit in with the roar and crackle. It was named 'The Burning of the Black Mill' and is still given as a set piece in piping competitions.

After Donald Glas's death, followed a year or two later by the death of his heir John, who had also been in the Edinburgh Tolbooth, Rob Roy felt he had a long score to pay off against the Scottish establishment and he did this unsparingly with a grim humour which endeared him to the common folk and will probably continue to delight them.

His mother having been a Campbell, and his brother and father having aided Glen Orchy to keep his Earldom, Rob had a foot in both camps, a great help to him in his exploits. For a time he dealt in black cattle and fell into trouble over a rogue of a partner, who absconded and left Rob to face his irate creditors. He was now, innocently perhaps, on the wrong side of the law. The Duke of Montrose, a Graham, was one of those who felt he had been cheated. He turned Rob's wife, Mary MacGregor of Comar, out of her house in wintry weather, with her young boys, in an effort to poind Rob's furniture and chattels. Rob now declared war on Montrose, for this injury, and of course was readily encouraged to do so by Argyll. The Grahams and Campbells, as I said earlier, were bitterly opposed, more so after the severities of the Civil War fifty years before. Argyll gave his distant relative, Rob, a house within his estates. The phrase is 'granted him wood and water'. When Argyll was taxed with this leniency towards such a desperado, he replied that his generosity was minimal compared with that of Montrose, who supplied Rob with bountiful and regular loads of meat; 'lifted' of course.

About this time Rob acquired the rocky estate of Craig Royston between Loch Katrine and Loch Lomond, a strategic point from which to conduct an extensive campaign of blackmail. It is thought that this word has nothing to do with colour, though black cattle were involved. It is an old word for protection money. The system was open to abuse. It was apt to turn into the sort of racket that goes on today. Pay up or else. But Rob was very skilful in recovering stolen cattle, for few thieves dared to argue with him. All the same, with property so insecure, the entire countryside near the Highland Line, in a broad belt across Scotland, about twenty miles wide, was rendered unproductive, and Rob got the blame for this general lawlessness, though there were many involved.

I do not think that I can do any justice in this short history to Rob's activities and adventures. I recommend those who are interested to read Scott's very long historical note on the MacGregors in the appendix to *Rob Roy*. The note runs to twenty thousand words, about half the length of this book; much of it is devoted to Rob Roy and his family. There are many other books on Rob, such as *Highland Constable*, by Hamilton Howlett, and the early collections I named in my introduction, by the Rev. Mr MacLeay.

In the risings of 1715 and 1719, Rob took over the leadership, though MacGregor of Balhaldie had been recognised as chief at a gathering in 1714, as I have said. Rob's action at Sheriffmuir, or lack of action, has often been criticised, but Hamilton Howlett defends his distant relative's record there. He believes he came too late to take effective action, and had too much sagacity to throw his men away on a forlorn hope. One of Rob's battalion is rumoured to have shown his lack of political interest by remarking that 'he was neither for King Shamus nor King Shordie but for King Spulzie (loot).' After this indecisive battle Rob and his men had a skirmish at Dunkeld with the Royal forces, from which they emerged losers, so they took over Falkland Palace in Fife, where they hibernated in all the crude comfort of early Scottish kings, and took a heavy toll of provisions from the 'Howe' of Fife.

I shall not expatiate farther on Rob's adventures. He was audacious, and physically far above normal ability. He was also shrewd and knew when he had better use discretion. This part of his nature perhaps he derived from the Campbells, for the MacGregors were not noted for being discreet. A business letter of his own composition is extant and shows he wrote a firm neat hand, grammatically correct, and had a grasp of money matters, as well as of the cash itself. His leisure reading was of high-class matter, judging by the journals and books he subscribed to, one of which was Keith's *History of Affairs of Church and State in Scotland*, published in Edinburgh in 1735, though Rob did not live to read it.

His exit is recorded quite as laconically as his entrance. The *Caledonian Mercury* of 9th January 1735 reported under Deaths:

'Robert MacGregor, (or Campbell) died at Inverloch-larigbeg (head of Loch Doine) parish of Balquhidder on Saturday was Se'night.' [That is, on the 28th December 1734.]

He was buried in the old Kirkyard of Balquhidder.

Scott believed that he died an aged man, but he was only 63 ('quite a young man' as my nonagenarian grandfather

David MacGregor remarked in my hearing). Perhaps his exertions in robbing the rich to help the poor (including himself) had prematurely aged him. In truth, however, he was one of the poor for, after his funeral expenses and small debts had been paid he left a personal estate of £275.13.4 (Scots) equal to £23 English, all to his wife Mary.

As to this misnaming of his wife as Helen, I have some contradictions to bring forward, on that and other misrepresentations. W. S. Crockett points out that she was named Mary, not Helen, and that she was of the Comar branch of the MacGregors. She was far from being the virago of Scott's novel. She was agreeable, domesticated, hospitable, musical and poetical.

Pursuing this point farther and completely demolishing this false character of Rob's wife, whom Scott likened to an Ate or classical female fiend, I would like to quote a correspondence which Sir Walter held with Mr. John Gregorson of Ardtornish, who had earlier supplied Scott with some information which the novelist acknowledges in his notes to *Rob Roy*. Scott had published in his 1818 (first) edition of *Rob Roy* that traditionally Dougal Ciar Mhor had committed the outrage at Glen Fruin. In the 'Advertisement to Edition, 1829 (January)' Scott corrected this false allegation when he revised his novels, though he was careful to specify certain fields wherein, as an artist, he did not feel justified in altering the unity of his creations by trivial corrections. But he nevertheless decided to publish 'various legends, family traditions, or obscure historical facts which have formed the groundwork of these novels.'

Presumably subsequent to the Edition of 1829 and (by the contents of Mr. Gregorson's letter) consequent on what he considered the inadequate corrections in that Edition, Scott received the following letter from Gregorson. I give a verbatim account of an extract.

'I beg leave also to state that the wife of Rob Roy who you represent as a horrid Fiend both by your work of fiction *and professed truth*, was a woman of totally different character.

It is a fact that in the days of her widowhood and adversity the tenant's wives of Craigroistan were in the habit of going to her with Kaine (rent in kind) Sheep, Hens, and eggs, and this tribute of respect they paid to her, as being herself a descendant of the MacGregors of Craigroistan as much as being the widow of Rob Roy who had only an ephemeral interest in the lands of Craigroistan.'

John Gregorson was Mary MacGregor's great-grand-nephew.

Knowing Sir Walter's generous character, we would expect that, had he been spared to recorrect an Edition of his novels, he would have included Gregorson's protest, but he died two years later, after a long breakdown, and his successors, until the days of W. S. Crockett, did not trouble to redress the grave injustice suffered by Mary MacGregor of Comar.

She bore Rob four sons, not five, as it is often repeated. They were James, Coll, Ronald and Robin Og (the younger); Duncan was an adopted relative. These sons were to offer the world an edifying picture of what it is to have wild men for ancestors, and to carry out their desperate courses in a world that professed to have outgrown such conduct.

Before I take final leave of Rob himself, I would like to nail another old lie, even though the *Encyclopaedia Britannica* (11th Edition), the *Dictionary of Natural Biography*, and other reference books make no effort to correct it, as far as I know. Crockett investigated this 'canard' very thoroughly; I refer to the tale that Rob Roy had been lodged in Newgate Prison, London, for treason, along with James, Lord Ogilvy, alleged also to be a Catholic. Crockett condemned this as unfounded rumour. There were no treason trials at that time, and Lord Ogilvy had been pardoned in 1725. Sir Walter Scott himself did not believe a word of it, or that Defoe had written the catchpenny chapbook, *The Highland Rogue* of 1723, which seems to have given rise to the scandal. What Scott said was quite a different thing, for anyone who could interpret good English. He said he 'could have *wished* Defoe had taken up the theme of Rob Roy.' What a story that would have made, a fitting companion for *Moll Flanders* published in 1721, the story of the whore who turned pious in her latter days. Rob Roy is said to have repented in his maturer years, too, and to have repaired to Father Drummond to confess his sins. Groans and cries of reproach were heard coming from the confessional, as Rob related his sins of commission (he apparently omitted nothing). Unluckily, that was before the age of bugging, or we should have had the basis of a first-rate autobiography with no holds barred.

Chapter 6. Rob Roy's Family.

Like their ancestors of the Glen Gyle line, especially their father and grandfather, Rob's four sons spent some part of their lives getting into, and out of, all sorts of political and legal trouble. James Mhor, or the Tall, as his father's heir, easily assumed the part of *fear-an-tighe*, or head of the household. Unlike Rob Roy, however, he appears to have been a person of uncontrollable temper. It has been said, on what evidence I do not know, that when his right to lead the MacGregors in the Forty-five was challenged by Glencarnoch, a MacGregor of another line, he behaved like a madman, and his rival broke off the argument in haste. It is understandable that, after ages of attempted dispersal and annulment, there should be insoluble problems about who should assume the place of honour in battle, and also, since the name was still proscribed in 1745, about whether a man who claimed to be a MacGregor was not a Campbell, a Murray, a Drummond, a Stewart or a Graham. James Mhor switched from being a Campbell, to being a Drummond, in 1729, to keep in with the Duke of Perth. He seemed never to be happy unless he was intriguing, and no person, perhaps not even himself, could guess what he would be planning next.

In the Forty-five rising he behaved very gallantly, along with his two brothers, Ronald and Robin Og. (Coll had died shortly after his father in 1735, aged about 31.) At Prestonpans the MacGregors were conspicuous by their wild charge and the carnage they inflicted with broadswords and cruder weapons such as Lochaber axes, or failing these, scythe-blades secured to long poles. On the retreat from Derby they again and again proved their worth, even in this long disheartening march. At Falkirk, where General Hawley found to his dismay that the cornered wild boar has tusks, along with the Camerons they fought in the centre of the line. When the clans reached the neighbourhood of Inverness the full significance of the gathering odds began to be realised. This is a much trodden field of Scottish history, and it is very fully documented now. It is hard to imagine how obscure the situation was to the actual combatants at the time. The Prince and his rather discordant staff had to send out parties to keep in touch with the advancing Cumberland, but it was equally important to find out the intentions of the large clans in the North who were antagonistic to the Jacobites, and who were being supplied by sea along the coasts of Easter Ross. Food for the half-starved clans under the Prince had also to be found.

The Jacobite army before the battle was 'diffused', and the conflict was forced upon them by sheer force of circumstances. They had attempted a night surprise on the Duke's forces but dawn had found them still some way off, so they had to retreat and were rapidly pursued to Drummossie Moor, where most of them were not adequately equipped or fed to stand up to cannons and the new use of bayonets. All this is too well known. What is not so well-known is that on the day of the battle the MacPhersons were in Badenoch, the Frasers in their own territory (the Lovat country), and 700 MacKinnons, MacGregors (under Glen Gyle), and Barisdale's forces, were in Sutherland confronting the MacKays and MacKenzies and other threatening forces. What difference these absent clans would have made is conjectural; but they were all noted for their panache in the onslaught. The idea still persists that Culloden was between Scots and English. A *Guide to the Battlefields of Britain and Ireland*, published recently, repeats this rubbish about Culloden. There were more clansmen in arms against Charles than for him. But had they known that their country was to be treated as a conquered land and subjected to pillage and rapine, they would have lived up to the ideal, (never realised), embodied in the Gaelic proverb 'The Clans of the Gaels shoulder to shoulder'. Although John MacGregor, the Prince's personal piper, was wounded on the field, the MacGregors have no clan gravestone on Culloden Moor, for the reason above given. They marched home, a defiant body, several hundred strong, banners flying, pipes playing, by the north-west shores of Loch Ness, with the Hanoverians following on the opposite shore, but powerless to attack them. They easily evaded Cumberland's forces and arrived back in Balquhidder and Glen Gyle, but ready to take to the hills on the threat of retribution.

The following month, May 1746, the *Scots Magazine* of that time reported that a party of the clan under Glen Gyle, Gregor Glun Dhubh, were out on the hills between Crieff and Dunkeld, engaged in highway robbery on 'publick money' (probably pay for the troops centred in Perth). Three hundred men from Brigadier Mordaunt's force set off in a vain search for these 'Children of the Mist'. In June a company of 700 troops entered Balquhidder and, failing to catch Glen Gyle or his men, they burned his house and all the MacGregor houses in the whole area and drove off their cattle. It is said that Ronald, Rob Roy's son advised the women not to retaliate in any way for the ruin of their homes, or they would incur the fate of the country folk in the Fort Augustus region, which I described briefly in my introduction, and which Smollett so graphically depicted in his poem 'The Tears of Scotland'. In this way we are spared having to include a Massacre of Balquhidder in our narrative.

After the Rising, James Mhor made his peace with the Government, after having been 'attainted for high treason with persons of more importance', as Scott says. Several of these Jacobite gentlemen perished on the scaffold in Tyburn, while others, notably the very estimable Lord Pitsligo, skulked about the countryside in the guise of beggars, dodging the redcoats but perfectly assured that none of their fellow-Scots would betray them. James was allowed to live unmolested in the Glen Gyle area and would have ended a longish life there, as Ronald did, if he had been content 'to jouk and let the jaw go by.'

But that was not his character. He incited his youngest brother Robin Og to take a wife and a fortune in one fell swoop, and this notorious abduction of Jean Key of Edinbelly is so well known, both in legal and lay history, that I need only give the bare outlines with a few original comments on the background, when I come to tell of Robin Og.

James was arrested because of his part in this abduction in 1750, but escaped from Edinburgh Castle through the daring subterfuge of Malie (Gaelic Maili), or May, MacGregor his daughter. She dressed herself as a cobbler and was admitted to his cell with her mother. A switch of clothes enabled James, (stooping like a cobbler to conceal his height), to escape and eventually reach France.

On the way he had met some British agents, and is accused of having done a package deal with them, offering to kidnap Alan Breck Stewart (under strong suspicion of guilt for the Appin murder), in return for a more favourable treatment of Robin Og, in custody in Edinburgh. As I have related earlier, the Glen Gyle MacGregors were related by blood to the Campbells of two important lines, and James Mhor had a family prejudice against the Stewarts, so he undertook the trepanning of Alan Breck with enthusiasm and sophisticated treachery. But Alan was forewarned by two friends, and escaped with some snuff boxes and other personal articles of MacGregor's, ready to be revenged on him more bloodily whenever he could. He had no need to; James took ill and died in a wretched apartment, quite romantically, in a certain sense, in a Bohemian quarter of Paris. His last letter, to Balhaldie, the Chief, is extant; Scott quotes a large section of it wherein James pleads for a job as a breeder and trainer of horses, or as a hunter, however menial and below his station of birth. His postscript asks for a loan of bagpipes on which he could solace himself by playing tunes of his beloved bens and glens. He died a week later. Alan Breck, immortalised in *Kidnapped*, was still alive in 1789 in Paris.

Ronald was also out in the Forty-five but was content to spend the next forty years farming mostly; but when in his prime, after the Rebellion, he is described as 'of Sir Duncan Campbell of Lochnell's Company' of militia. He died in 1786, four years after Clan Gregor, like the other clans, was actually permitted to resume the wearing of its distinctive tartan.

Robin Og was tried, after some delay in catching him, for the abduction of Jean Key, but, before this alleged rape, he had committed a manslaughter by shooting a relative as he was ploughing on land that Robin claimed was his mother's. He managed to escape punishment by joining the British army. He fought at Fontenoy in 1745, where the Duke of Cumberland and the whole British army surrendered to Marshal Saxe, the most ignominious defeat up to that date in all British military history. Cumberland was to prove more successful the following year, glorying in butchery of British prisoners. Robin Og was exchanged after Fontenoy and the mortification of that surrender perhaps induced him to enlist with the Jacobites; with no greater success, but more honour.

Condemned to death for the abduction of Jean Key, his last day on earth dawned on 14th February, St. Valentine's Day, a pretty ironic time to die because of a mismanaged love affair. I now quote the account of his execution, from the *Caledonian Mercury*, a journal printed in Edinburgh.

'He was very genteelly dressed, behaved with great decency and declared he died an unworthy member of the Church of Rome and still further he attributed all his misfortunes to his swerving two or three years ago from that communion.'

As Marvell wrote of the execution of Charles I,

'He nothing common did or mean
Upon that memorable scene.'

On the way to the scaffold in the Grassmarket, Edinburgh, he had to pass the very spot where, exactly a century and a half before, Alastair MacGregor and eleven of his clan had been unjustly executed; we have no means of knowing whether

Robin Og was aware he was so close to that unhallowed spot, though he may have thought bitterly that he was suffering some injustice himself, in view of the controversial evidence in his trial.

The failure of the '45 rising was followed by repression in all fields, including the law courts, for over thirty years. The face of Scottish 'justice', as well as of English, was cold and hostile towards anyone of Jacobite leanings. It is salutary to compare and contrast two cases of abduction, one a few years before the '45, the other a few years after.

In 1737 Donald MacLachlan, son of a bailie of Inveraray, carried off Christian MacArthur from a boarding-school in that burgh. He took her to Ireland and married her. He was fined £20 Sterling.

In 1753, Robin MacGregor was tried for a similar offence. The evidence was so conflicting (as there was some weighty evidence of Jean Key's connivance at her abduction, including a very endearing love-letter) that the jury absolved him of two of the main charges, and could not agree that he was guilty of a capital crime. However, after a very lengthy course of legal quibbling, which reflects very badly on the judiciary's sense of fair play, sentence of death was passed exactly to the very calendar day nineteen years after Rob Roy's death (though, owing to the correction of the Gregorian calendar in 1752 it was about a fortnight out).

As he passed down the Bow he read from a volume of Gother's works. John Gother was a Roman Catholic protagonist of whom Dryden said, 'He is the only man beside myself who knows how to write the English language.' It is strange that Gother's name is not to be found in any list of English men of letters, yet his works were in Rob Roy's household along with works in Gaelic and other languages.

Tradition, which persisted for long after his death, reports that when the hangman tried to appropriate Robin's clothes, (which were his best) as his customary due, Malie MacGregor, the same woman of spirit who had secured her father's escape, turned on the executioner in a fury, screaming, 'You've already done enough and won't be allowed to touch any part of my uncle's dress!' To back up her words, she paid the hangman in his own coin, in a manner of speaking, by 'swinging him off' on his back across the causeway, to the great glee of the Edinburgh mob, to whom any hangman was an object of execration.

Robin's body was carried to Balquhidder, clothed as it was, with an adequate guard of MacGregors, considerably reinforced at Linlithgow by those whose record of lawlessness was such that they did not venture within a day's march of Edinburgh. Laments were piped most of the long journey of two days, with a final coronach as they laid Robin Og to rest, close by the very rough stone that marks his father's grave.

So ends the tale of Rob Roy's immediate descendants. Many people claim direct descent from him, now at a distance of a quarter of a millennium or about ten generations. Some of these claims are authentic and it can be proved that a large number of men and women are in his line. For example, as I mentioned earlier in another respect, I am at present in correspondence with Mr. Andrew MacEwan, of Stockton Springs, Maine, USA who is a direct descendant of James Mhor MacGregor of Glen Gyle through his son John, who emigrated to Canada. Mr. Hamilton Howlett, author of *Highland Constable*, also claims direct descent. Although I have never claimed this distinction (being pretty certain I am not directly descended, but that my family were Glen Gyle MacGregors), I have several times been quoted as claiming it. Apparently no amount of categorical denials has any effect, once a popular cry gets up.

Chapter 7. End of an Old Song.

Culloden marked the end of effective Jacobite resistance to the Hanoverians, but it did not suppress all feelings of revolt. The Stuarts still plotted to regain the British throne. Sir Walter Scott described an abortive attempt at a new rising in *Redgauntlet*. This novel takes its name from Sir Robert Hugh

Redgauntlet, a character based on the notorious Grierson of Lag, a persecutor of the Covenanters. He was of the Clan Gregor, his family having moved south during their earliest persecutions to become lairds in the parish Dunscore in West Dumfriesshire. The 15th century tower of Lag, their seat, now in ruins, was not far from Ellisland, where Burns spent a few happy years.

Prince Charles Edward visited London in 1750, in the forlorn hope of enlisting his Tory friends. His presence was known to the government, but no attempt was made to arrest him.

The following short extract from Dr. King's *Anecdotes*, recently reprinted by John Murray, will reveal something of the Young Pretender's character as seen by the friendly but unflattering eye of a strong Jacobite.

'September 1750, I received a note from my Lady Primrose who desired to see me immediately. As soon as I waited on her, she led me into her dressing-room and presented me to — [The Pretender].

'As to his person he is tall and well-made but stoops a little, perhaps due to the great fatigue which he underwent in his northern expedition. He has a handsome face and good eyes; but in polite society he would not pass for a genteel man ... I never heard him express any noble or benevolent sentiments, the certain indications of a great soul and a good heart; or discover any sorrow or compassion for the misfortunes of so many worthy men who had suffered in his cause. But the most odious part of his character is his love of money, a vice which I do not remember to have been imputed by our historians to any of his ancestors, and is a certain index of a base and little mind ... To this spirit of avarice may be added his insolent manner of treating his immediate dependants, very unbecoming a great prince and a sure prognostic of what might be expected from him if ever he acquired sovereign power.'

What was the condition of the clansmen who had risen? It is too well-known, but the interpretations put upon it are still so controversial that little hope can be entertained of a just assessment. It perplexed the worthy men of the latter half of the 18th century to explain the strange and serious phenomenon that the Highlanders presented. An unbiased traveller in the 1770–80 period described the general picture as antique, savage, poor and picturesque. Even the relatively well-ordered burgh of Inveraray, which was not in the suppressed area, was described as a straggling township of thatched hovels apart, of course, from one or two well-built ducal edifices. Inverness, the centre of the rebel country, a generation after the massacre of prisoners in its streets, was apparently so ruinous as to seem on the verge of extinction. When better houses and shops began to be built, no applicants came forward to act as town scavenger, an example of pride and poverty. Starvation, literal death by hunger, was common when harvests were bad. The once fertile province of Moray had so far fallen into bad condition from its mediaeval prosperity that it could not maintain its native population, and even well into the 19th century one in ten of the population of Elgin was on the pauper's roll.

Adam Smith, of *Wealth of Nations* fame, wrote these terrible words, 'A half-starved Highland woman frequently bears twenty children. It is not uncommon for a Highland mother to have borne twenty children and not to have two alive.'

There were not wanting efforts to bring some sort of economic prosperity to the Highlands in the form of weaving-mills and other productive schemes. Many translations of religious works, including the Old and New Testaments, were made into Gaelic and widely distributed; over 30,000 were printed from 1770 to 1790. Yet the population declined in areas not affected by the savage clearances, and, of course, Gaelic declined also.

The truth is never simple even when discoverable, but a good deal of it can be expressed in the saying, 'Where there is no vision the people perish.' History is full of such decadent societies. The brutalities of four centuries had finally emasculated the Celts, both of Ireland and the Scottish Highlands, the last insular remnants of a great culture. The Clan Gregor had been conspicuous in its fierce opposition to Norman-Anglo feudalism, but its own brand of clan feudalism, in some way just as tyrannical, had been crushed. The post-Culloden Highlands bore the same relationship to the old clan system as a yoke-ox does to a free-ranging bull. I need not attempt an analysis of the phenomenon which puzzled the anxious economists of Adam Smith's day. My own great-grandfather, after a miserable youth in Strathspey, toiling with a hungry soil and working hard at setting up watermills, and even making spinning-wheels, did a one-man clearance to Glasgow where he suffered even more severely, domestically and industrially, at the time of the 1820 strikes and brutal suppressions. The MacNabs, led by their chief, The MacNab, emigrated en masse to Canada. Every week saw crowds of Highlanders of all ages and conditions taking ship at the Broomielaw, and at all sorts of anchorages off the West Coast, to set off on the perilous trip to America, often to face conditions worse at the outset than they had left.

In 1757 two regiments were formed as an experiment to use the military skill of the Highlanders in the Seven Years War in North America. It was a scheme which had been proposed exactly twenty years before by Duncan Forbes of Culloden: but although it had all the elements which would have obviated the Forty-five rising, as well as providing efficient troops for the continental wars, it was turned down by Parliament because of a fear that the Highland troops, armed with muskets, bayonet and artillery would conquer England.

By 1774 it was still illegal to wear the tartan or even to play the pipes and display any of the insignia of Celtic life. But what annoyed the MacGregors particularly was the continuing proscription of their name when this law had been long a dead letter. For example a Baron MacGregor, who died in 1734, owned an estate at Newhaven, near Edinburgh and was well respected under that name, especially in Leith. Yet the eccentric minister of the first Gaelic chapel in Edinburgh, opened in 1769, had to call himself the Rev. Joseph Robertson, his mother's clan name, because he could not hold office as a MacGregor.

In 1774 a venerable gentleman, who lived at Gosport and had served first in the Black Watch during the early reign of George II, and subsequently in the Middlesex Regiment of Militia, prepared a petition to George III, imploring him to release the MacGregors from their long annulment of name. His name was Gregor MacGregor of Inverarderan, and his by-name was Gregor Boidheach or the Handsome. R. L. Stevenson introduces him, without naming him, in Alan Breck Stewart's account of the three Highland Gentlemen who were invited to give a display of broadsword before the king in London. The king gave each three guineas and Alan Breck claimed that it was probably his ancestor who, to show his quality, had given the whole sum to the door keeper as he left the palace. Gregor was certainly one of the three. He was not in the Forty-five, unlike his namesake and relative Gregor MacGregor, Glun Dhubh of Glen Gyle. He was therefore more likely to be listened to by Parliament.

His suit was successful. On November 29th 1774 the house debated the repeal of the old Act of Proscription, begun in 1603, uplifted in 1661, renewed in 1693. Gregor MacCallum VcGregor VcDougall VcCallum MacGregor died full of years, on 4th February, 1779 at Gosport, and to him all MacGregors ought to pay tribute, and if they ever visit Gosport they ought to lay a wreath of Scots pine on his grave, though I do not know if anyone there can point it out. But, in order to make his petition carry more weight this veteran offered to raise a regiment of MacGregors, to be officered by their own chieftains, to proceed to suppress the American rebels. I am filled with admiration for the magnanimity of the 'rebels', for the bi-centenary of this Repeal last year was most prominently observed by a visit to Scotland of two hundred American MacGregors and friends. However, Gregor's honour is upheld, for he excused himself, from helping to raise this clan regiment, on account of his advanced age and infirmity.

The act permitting the wearing of the tartan and accessories was not put into force until 1782, which shows the panic that the Government had been in, nearly forty years before. Apparently the tartan had a supernatural power not normally inherent in woollen cloth. In *Old and New Edinburgh*, a three-volume work by James Grant on all sorts of tradition of that city, the Rev. Joseph Robertson MacGregor, mentioned above, 'dressed himself up in a full suit of MacGregor tartan' the very day that he was legally permitted to do so, and paraded both Old and New Edinburgh in this startling rig-out. Grant gives the date at 1787, but I think this must be a printer's error; unless there was the same amount of delay in the Circumlocution Department Offices as we have grown to accept today. As the City Guard, the 'Black Banditti' of Robert Fergusson's poems, were all veteran Highland soldiers and part of the 1,500 members of MacGregor's congregation of porters, sedan-chair men and caddies, there was no way of putting a stop to the Saturnalia that was celebrated in Auld Reekie that night. MacGregor was celebrated for his convivial supervision of funerals, marriages and baptisms. Nevertheless, when a grand parade of militia took place twenty years later, to grace His Majesty's Birthday, Joseph was there, this time in more sober habit, to give the multitude his blessing. The Almighty has had worse priests.

Act or no Act, the year before the tartan was set free, in 1781, as I mentioned in my introduction, at the great Falkirk Tryst, the biggest sheep and cattle market in Britain, the piping championship was taken by Patrick MacGregor. I cannot imagine him winning it, unless dressed in the tartan. From 1784, the first year of the Edinburgh Piobaireachd Meetings, when John MacGregor II was champion, until 1812 (twenty-nine years inclusive), eleven championships were won by MacGregors. But the strange fact emerges, on scanning the lists, in David Webster's *Scottish Highland Games*, that from that year, with the exception of 1855, when John MacGregor VI championed the Northern Meeting at Inverness, the Clan Gregor pipe is are entirely absent from the Championship list. The ancient MacGregor piping school, as I wrote earlier, was at Drumcharaig, near Fortingal and was in full blast long after the legendary MacCrimmons had played themselves into Tir nan Og, the Celtic Paradise. It is quite likely that Drumcharaig was abandoned as a school when (like Rob Roy on his deathbed) they had piped their last lament 'Cha till mi tuilich', I shall return no more. Maybe their American descendants can be heard each year at the Annual Highland Gathering on Grandfather Mountain, U.S.A. or in Nova Scotia, though I can vouch that several descendants live in Scotland.

The MacGregor tunes are still well-known, particularly the 'MacGregors Gathering', a Gaelic air altered and set to rather fustian words by Scott. 'The Rout of Glen Fruin' and 'The Burning of the Black Mill' and perhaps 'The Braes of Glen Orchy' (with Campbell orchestration) are still used. 'Loch Lomond', universally known, was composed by a MacGregor, under sentence of death in Carlisle Castle, in 1746. It represents a Celtic belief that the ghost of the slain travelled under earth to haunt the place dearest in memory. The condemned man was a native of Glen Endrick, on the south-east of Loch Lomond. The original words of course were in Gaelic, with internal rhymes. This should be remembered when people, ignorant of this poetical subtlety, condemn the song because it does not have end rhymes.

'How are the mighty fallen!' The marching song of the marauding bands of MacGregors, which struck terror into all hearers, was none of the above. It was a lively chant which has been so far reduced in effect that is now a street-song for many Scottish children. It goes by the name, 'In and out the dusty bluebells'.

The fate of Auld Nick in Scotland symbolises that of the MacGregors. Once the last word in bogeys, he is now a figure of fun. He is no longer used to terrify waukrife bairns into shutting their eyes, as he once was, along with 'Jenny wi the Airn Teeth' and 'Jenny Kilfunk', her demon sister. The MacGregors are also comical. Dr. MacGregor is referred to as a shadowy predecessor in *Dr. Finlay's Casebook*; he, or another man of the same name, goes around Dunblane on his tricycle in Will Fyfe's song, 'Dr. MacGregor and his Wee Black Bag'. An out-dated collection of Glaswegian everyday life in Edwardian days, when I also holidayed at Rothesay in my sailor-suit, is entitled *Wee MacGreegor* and catches the eye with Hassall's cartoon of a wee Glaswegian. In the (1903) *Glasgow Poets*, a lavishly produced anthology, or better described as a potpourri, (literally a 'rotten-pot'), there are strange bed-fellows to be found, from excellence to putrescence. The book ends with about the sickest joke ever printed, 'The Lament of Dougal MacGregor', which no doubt is a good example of an Irish-inspired burlesque similar in morbid humour to 'The Night before Larry was Stretched'. I dare say I can laugh at myself with all the rest, as a MacGregor; and I do. But, behind the ridicule, I do not need to be a very subtle psychologist to analyse an archaic fear. However 'I'll let that flee stick to the wa',' as Rob Roy said, 'and when it's dry the dirt will rub oot.' I shall show in my concluding chapter that if the MacGregors went out with a whimper and a giggle in Scotland, they went out with a bang, still reverberating, elsewhere.

Summing-up.

1. *A Backward Glance.*

I think that my reader, if he or she has had the patience to continue with me to this distance, may have been convinced that I have tried my best to get at the truth, and yet to present a flowing narrative, with slight pauses to digress into interesting incidents. I have also written this story with some feeling, as I promised, or warned, in my apology. I have been compelled to do this because, as a MacGregor, I am inextricably bound up in my subject.

At the risk of disappointing some of my clan, I must remark that, compared with the qualities of devotion to tradition, endurance, and courage in the face of every adversity, the claim to a royal lineage (though I have substantially established it, both for chiefs and clan) is relatively unimportant. A man's a man for a' that.

If, however, we mean by royalty, not the petty eminence of rank, brought about by an accident of birth and circumstance, but the nobility which mankind is too often prone to ignore, unless it is accompanied by sounding brass and conspicuous insignias, then, as a clan, we have every justification, having 'tholed our assizes' to proclaim "*S Rìoghail mo Dhrèam*'. This has been best said by Thomas Browne, 'There is surely a piece of divinity in us, something that was before the elements, and owes no homage unto the sun.'

I need not excuse the great historical stretch of my story. Indeed, had I had access to records, which, if ever committed to writing, have long since perished, I should have extended my history much farther back. As it is, whether with or without a perspective glass, we can turn about, and from the advantage of present time, we can look across the wide and varied landscape which the Space-Time Continuum provides on Earth, and, with ease or with effort, according to our powers of mental concentration, we can make out an interminable caravan moving from the vastnesses of the infinite waste towards us. At times it disappears as it threads its way among foothills, 'bad-lands', and thickets, to emerge, often drastically reduced in force; frequently as in the present instance which forms this book, the mists of storms obscure its progress, and the deadlier pall arising from the devastations of enemies and the sulphurous fumes of battles. Then, as the individual figures emerge and become distinguishable, we associate their struggle and varying fortunes with our own, and involve ourselves in their fate. They come so close that we see the whites of their eyes and with a gasp of recognition are face to face with men and women who, by all the blind odds in creation, should have been dead, rotten, and forgotten, in some wilderness of primordial heather and rock, ages before, but who, perhaps guided by ancestral gods have won triumphantly through.

Then, surprisingly, this procession of persistent clansfolk begins to disperse. To leave this figure of speech and come to reality, they were largely forced to leave their native heath for all manner of reasons, apart from scarcely relenting persecution. The clearances of 18th and 19th centuries were only partly to blame. The same expelling forces effectively swept bare the great moors of the Southern Uplands. Lack of opportunity to fulfil ambitions, however humble, was too often the cause of their leaving Scotland, a fertile mother but an indigent nurse. This still continues. It is tragic that many Highlanders, MacGregors only a small minority, had to make their reputations amongst alien people and to rise to fame that never reached the ears of Scotland, or, if by chance it did, was treated with indifference, or jealous distaste, in the land of their birth.

The continuing achievements of these clansmen, in every human sphere, derive from their early origins. All researchers are agreed that the body of the Clan Gregor, and closely associated clans, sprang from monastic forebears, or more precisely from the ecclesiastic communities founded by St. Fillan, seconded by Columban monks and secured in succession by Finghin or Findanus, traditionally the grandson of King Gregorius Magnus. These early ecclesiasts were not milksops, they were men of terrifying zeal, courage and intellect, whom no toil could discourage and who trembled at no lions in the path. When their rights were unjustly infringed, even though they had discarded their clerical habits, their characters were permanently fixed through training and birth in all the succeeding generations, and they emerged from persecution, (political, religious, or an amalgam of both), with an unbroken spirit, refusing to quit their ancient territories, and ready, when the ban was lifted, after 'an unconscionable time', to devote their considerable energies to the advancement of all human activities.

The past could never be forgotten, the less so because it was a vindication of injustice overturned, against overwhelming odds. As Joseph Anderson says, 'Even throughout the time when the clan were declared outlaws and social outcasts, incurring prejudices against them, many MacGregors had occupied positions requiring education, ability and character. In the appalling circumstances this was scarcely to be expected of them.' Whether they could face success and recognition with the same equanimity as had enabled them to endure the extremes of persecution, was to be proved after the lifting of the penal acts against them.

I would like, near the finale, to anticipate critics, (presuming, in the present torrent of publications, that they have had time to read past the title and the author's name before passing judgement): their query may well be put, 'Why bring up the past centuries of evil-doing?' This is the general objection to any resurrection of dry bones, and doubtless, when Ezekiel was asked by the Lord, 'Son of man, can these bones live?' he was very dubious when he answered, 'O Lord

God thou knowest.' Looking around at the very many and very dry bones that litter the glens and straths of Scotland in the form of industrial waste, slums, man-made deserts once teeming with clansmen and now marked by the larachs of long abandoned homes, it is very little to the purpose to ask 'Can these bones live?' We ought to know very well from the past that God can put his spirit upon any resolute people 'to come up out of their graves and be placed in their own land.' 'Even in our ashes live our wonted fires', is the appropriate line in the burial-ground of Clan Gregor in Glen Gyle.

2. The Failure of Proscriptions.

Defying Hegel's cynical aphorism, which I quoted at the beginning, about the inability of nations to learn from the past, even their own, I shall not let the lesson of history go again by default, as it did in the 16th and 17th centuries, at severe cost to Clan Gregor, and as it has, universally, done again, many times, in my own lifetime.

The most famous historical proscriptions, precisely by that name, were the proscriptions of Sulla in the first century BC when that general, returning from his conquests in Asia Minor, overthrew his rivals and gained absolute power in the Roman Republic. Instead of exercising mercy, either from policy or goodwill, and thereby enlisting the support of all his former enemies, notably the ancient states of Etruria, Samnium and Lucania, he devastated these regions, massacred whole populations, proscribed many tribes, took over their territories and gave them to his own legionaries. He had no regard for the future of the republic which never recovered from his reign of terror and which was degraded politically into an Empire soon after. The immediate evils were the revolts of slaves under Spartacus, who ranged over all Italy with 70,000 'broken men', burning, robbing and murdering until their tortured corpses finally lined the Appian Way upon miles of crucifixes. Worst of all for the economy of the future, the land, bereft of its original farming people, became unproductive and drove the Rome of imperial days to depend on imported grain. Manpower, based on the sturdy Italianate peasantry, was in such short supply, owing to Sulla's combined policies of landrobbing and proscription, that the legions had to be mainly recruited from barbarian tribes. These armies often elected and instated Emperors of their own races and led to the imperceptible decay of Rome.

George Buchanan, the austere tutor of James VI, was the most learned classical scholar of his age. He certainly instructed James in the history of classical antiquity. James nonetheless, a typical Stuart, though given the very best advice, invariably following his personal promptings, chose to act on the opposite principles. (Charles Edward was notoriously prone to do this, placing the wisdom of Clementina Walkinshaw above Solomon's.) Despite the example of Rome, James VI, when he could have started off his United Kingdom by setting the clock of history back with advantage, by restoring the ancient rights in his three kingdoms, deliberately pursued Sullan measures in the Highlands, most severely against the MacGregors, but also against other clans. This policy was followed by Charles, 'that unfeathered thing, his son', then renewed by the Dutch husband of Mary Stuart and again by Anne, the last of the line. The Hanoverians took over the task and employed legions of Hessian barbarians in the Highlands, as in America, to butcher the rebels. The native Highlanders, seeking a way to escape semi-starvation, were recruited and spent in England's expansionist wars, and when the survivors returned they were deprived of their territories. While the recruitment of Highland troops formed the majority of Scotland's soldiers in the Napoleonic wars, Skye alone raising 10,000 men in that time, when it came to the Crimean campaigns the clearances had been so effective that the majority of the 'Highland' regiments were composed of Irishmen and Englishmen.

Professor Proinsias MacCana, of the chair of Welsh in University College, Dublin, writes of the Celts, who formed one of the great branches of the world's population, dominating Europe and extending to Asia Minor and the British Isles, that 'their unity was one of culture rather than of race'; that the European Celts have been absorbed into other political groups and that the British Celts are 'in sadly reduced circumstances'. Yet, despite their fall from fortune they still maintain their ancient traits, noted by classical writers two thousand years ago, of 'eloquence, lyric genius, volatile temperaments, prodigality, reckless bravery, ebullience, contentiousness and so on'.

But these qualities, from excellent to bad, have been sadly dispersed; sadly for Britain, that is, like the good old English virtues of fair play, truth-telling and debt-paying that were expelled to form America by the same royal ukases of James.

J. H. Burton comments on the gains to foreign lands that followed Scotland's losses: 'how dreary a thing it is that a community should have to dismiss the choice of its children from its own bosom ...' He then, over a century ago, wonders 'whether we are to have a struggle with another great power which several Scotsmen helped to consolidate?' The great power with which we had struggled was France, which had been helped in many ways by Scots both during and after the Auld Alliance. Armed with hindsight we know to our cost that Burton's wondering came to grim reality in the two German wars and in the subsequent uncertainty of Russian intentions. Thousands of Scots helped the military consolidation of Prussia. Names like Mackensen (MacKenzie) (whose leadership defeated the 'Russian steamroller' in 1915, and indirectly caused the Revolution) keep cropping up in German history.

Here I would like to give instances of these achievements from the Clan Gregor, as that is most relevant. The other Scots clans and families are fully represented in Burton's *The Scot Abroad*.

3. Wide Influence of MacGregors.

When we viewed with apprehension the increasing power and ubiquity of the Russian navy, how many of us remembered that the creator of Russian sea-power was a MacGregor? Peter the Great had begun the establishment of naval strength, but it was in the early days of Catherine, his notorious successor, that application was made by the Russians to the British Navy, for officers to improve their naval tactics and equipment, in competition with the Swedes and Turks. Samuel Greig, of Inverkeithing, whose name had been assumed from MacGregor, was the son of a skipper. He was one of the officers chosen. He advanced rapidly, a progress he would not have made in the British Navy at that period as we know from the circumstances which led to the execution of Byng. Greig was, by reason of personal courage and skill, advanced to Commodore. In the great trial of strength between the Swedes and Russians at Hogeland in 1788, he commanded the Russians. This was perhaps the most 'remarkable of sea-battles, not only for the determined and obstinate fighting on both sides, but for being fought in a storm, and in a narrow sea full of shoals, currents and other perils.' Burton had difficulty in getting any information about the battle, because of Russian tight-lipped diplomacy, but he eventually found a pro-Swedish German account which gave particulars of that very bloody sea-fight, in which Greig received his death wound, and which, though claimed by both sides as a victory, put an end to Swedish ambitions in Europe; Greig was given such a barbarically gorgeous funeral by the Empress, that it was described by every newspaper in Europe, though I should be surprised to learn that it had been reported in Scotland. This battle was fully as decisive in world politics as Trafalgar, as we now know, but neither the names of Samuel Greig (Chevalier of the Russian Orders of St. Andrew, Alexander Nevski, St. George, St. Vladimir and St. Anne) nor yet of Hogeland, are to be found as articles in the *Encyclopaedia Britannica*. He seems in process of being suppressed, just like his eponym Gregor MacDungal.

Canning, the British Premier, claimed that his policies encouraged the 'New World to redress the balance of the Old', by which he meant that he viewed with approval the numerous bodies of British military men who, with veteran experience, went to South America to help the rebels oust the Spanish and Portuguese. One of the most famous of these, Bolívar's right-hand man, who fought in such sanguinary battles as the second battle of Carabobo 1821, which decided the fate of an area larger than France and Great Britain together, was Gregor MacGregor, already mentioned as the grandson of Gregor Glun Dhubh the nephew of Rob Roy. Despite his involvement in a second Darien Scheme fully as disastrous as the first, he was awarded honours and a pension by the grateful Venezuelans. General MacGregor is still remembered in Caracas; in Edinburgh, apart from a certain obloquy associated with the unforgivable Scots sin of financial failure, he is consigned to Limbo.

Among those who served their own country abroad is the Father of the British Army Medical Corps, Sir James MacGrigor. His conscientious labours and organisation procured the praises of one of Napoleon's chief officers in the Peninsular War; he remarked 'The British forces are under sanitary discipline; the French army is a perambulating brothel.'

On the aggressive side the MacGregors ought to have been represented by Sir Colin Campbell, Lord Clyde, probably the most pugnacious officer on record, in miscellaneous wars, of a variety of moral justification; from the crossing of the Bidassoa river in the Basque country under very heavy fire where he was wounded, but where Wellington beat Soult, to the 'Thin Red Line' in the Crimea, famous in story and picture. In between, he bloodily suppressed a West Indian revolt, enforced the debauchery of the Chinese in the Opium War, and, when he was past retiral age, advanced at the head of the Highland troops, to the second relief of Lucknow. His christened name was Colin MacLiver, a MacGregor sept, but due to a misunderstanding when, aged sixteen, he was being enlisted by his uncle, Campbell, as an ensign in the 9th Foot, he was wrongly entered. The facts are well authenticated, but once again, some people have not yet heard of the Repeal of the Proscriptive Acts two centuries ago.

These are very wide foreign fields where the energy of the restored MacGregors has been put to good account. I could quote examples ad nauseam; but I shall now pass to the even more spacious spheres. A dynasty of MacGregors started with James Gregory of Aberdeen, inventor of the reflecting telescope, which permitted the human mind to explore the remotest depths of space before the modern techniques of radar astronomy. In his line arose several Gregorys, brilliant if irascible doctors of medicine, one of whom, the 'Starving Doctor', also James, bestowed on suffering mankind the bitter stomachic remedy of 'Dr. Gregory's Mixture'. Inner space was their study, and very few were the F.O.s* that they failed to identify.

Another Aberdeen family, compelled to adopt the name Greig, fled to Norway after Culloden to pursue a commercial career. The second generation gave birth to Edvard Grieg, who through the medium of Norse tradition and landscape imparted anew the natural lyricism of his clan.

Against my nature I am almost forced to conclude that the spiritual energy of Celtic Scotland which is essential to the continued welfare of the state, irrespective of bureaucratic fostering, has been dissipated by centuries of prodigal misrule. Still, I do not wish to end this story with a dying fall and go out like the 'souch o' an auld sang.' Resurgences of nations have occurred in the past, are taking place now, and doubtless will continue. Some of them have prospects of success much less than Scotland finds within its grasp. I trust that the Clan Gregor will be found on the side of the angels this time.

* Foreign Objects.

INDEX